Inside the Cyclone

A story of ups and downs

Dan Roach

The events and conversations in this book have been set down
to the best of the author's ability, although some names and
details may have been changed to protect the privacy of
individuals.

First paperback edition October 2020

Cover photography by Tony Mcdowell

ISBN 979-8-6698-7811-5 (paperback)

danroachauthor.wordpress.com

facebook.com/danroachauthor

For Nan…

"There's no such word as can't." –

Harriet Joan Yates 1921 - 2015

Contents

Foreword

One of the pleasures of my job as editor of Microlight Flying is the quality of stories and photographs I get from readers, which is why I always open an e-mail from Danny with a sense of happy anticipation.

I'm never disappointed. As anyone who's read either his pieces in MF, or on his blog or Facebook page, will already be fans of his sense of humour and the talent of a born writer to turn ordinary experiences - if you could ever describe flying a microlight, or indeed Danny, as ordinary - into extraordinary prose.

I've also always had a soft spot for his stories about Harriet, his AX3, since I learned in one, and had a half share in one which was a joy to fly. It's an aircraft which encapsulates the very essence of microlighting which we all had when we started to learn - to fly simply and affordably, and to feel at one with the sky when we finally made it there.

Even better, he goes one step further in this and delves into the fascinating history of the type, from its predecessor as the Weedhopper through epic flights across the North Sea to Norway, its surprising military career where it was used as a fun aircraft by RAF pilots who loved it, and for good measure some of the jaunts and japes it got into at the hands of some of the many pilots who flew it and also loved it, as we all did, who had the privilege to fly one.

The result is not only a wonderful personal story of one man's dream to fly, but a fascinating history of a lovely little aircraft.

Geoff Hill

Introduction

In many ways, it was a far from perfect morning to go flying. I was a little agitated having had a longer than expected journey north to the airfield, the M6 car park living up to its name in several places which added to my already edgy mind. With a couple of miles to go I had received a text from James, my instructor, to ask if I was still coming as I was late.

Turning into Tarn Farm, or Rossall Field as it is now called, I arrived at the home of Attitude Airsports in a hail of gravel and dust from the hard braking applied to ensure I didn't continue my current course that would take me through the side of the caravan, err, Pilots' Lounge…

I jumped out and saw, to my dismay, James taxying up the side of the hangar in his Nynja, presumably getting ready for the next lesson.

Damn.

My wrist buzzed, and I glanced disconsolately at the screen of my watch, which informed me I had received a text message. Leaning in through the open car door whilst trying not to cough on the still gravel infused air I retrieved my phone.

Another text from James.

"Get her out mate, we've still got time."

My mood lifted slightly and retreated a few notches back down the driving stress-o-meter.

Earlier that day, I had been greeted by a cold and breezy May morning as I awoke and checked the tree (think local wind sock) out of my bedroom window.

It was still.

Good.

I had then looked at the Terminal Aerodrome Forecast (TAF) which reassuringly read VRB/02 (Variable wind direction, 2 knots wind speed).

Good.

So, with these favourable conditions, the idea of losing out again on this potential first flight in Yankee Lima was unthinkable to me. Luckily, it seemed that things were turning around in my favour.

And so, running into the hangar I skipped around YL unclipping the bungees that hold on the tarpaulins I use to prevent the birds from using her as a convenient target for toilet practice, or something like that.

"Calm down mate – we've got plenty of time, get your breath."

I looked up to see James standing in front of me with a pre-flight brew warming his hands.

I took a breath and then after checking the wingtips were clear I pulled Yankee Lima out of the hangar.

Today was to be THE day.

Noticing the airframe twitching around a bit, I stole a reluctant glance at the windsock which was now currently moving about so much that it reminded me of my nine-year-old daughter's limitless energy first thing in the morning; if I could find a way to bottle that I would solve the world's clean energy problem straight away! Anyway, despite the increasingly strong wind it was, at least, fairly straight down the nearly 500 metres of runway 02, the longest runway for this, my first flight in my own aeroplane.

An aeroplane I had now owned for nearly a year. It had been one thing after another that had prevented me from flying her. Either the weather was unsuitable, I was not available, James was not available, the weather, then the permit expired, the weather, oh and did I mention?

The weather…

As a qualified and current National Private Pilots' Licence (NPPL) holder already I had no legal need to go up with an instructor in Yankee Lima but I figured only fools take unnecessary risks and I didn't want to be a fool, or a dead fool for that matter, so I had (im)patiently waited for the stars to align and had been beginning to wonder if Yankee Lima and I were destined to remain on the ground and never fly together.

Pulling on the wooden two-bladed propeller, I manoeuvred her into wind and she settled down a bit.

"Ok," I breathed and leaned into the cockpit to connect the radio and headsets.

Beginning with the engine, I did my pre-flight walkaround. Everything seemed to be attached as it should be and nothing appeared to be loose. This check was especially important as it was the aforesaid nine-year-old and her elder sister who had helped me attach the wings to Yankee Lima's fuselage in the weeks after her arrival by road. So, with the airframe looking good I took a quick look at the tyres and confirmed they still had air in them and then glanced in the back to note that there were around 30 litres of fuel visible in the twin tanks.

"I'm happy," I confidently declared to James.

Now it was time to 'fold' ourselves into the cockpit. Anyone who has ever installed themselves (for that is what it feels like) into the cockpit of an AX3 will understand what I mean by 'fold'. I'm quite agile and flexible for a 40-something man, but it took me quite a while to get the hang of it. And whatever you do, don't go flying in an AX3 with anyone unless you don't mind getting cosy with them as you will definitely get close during the insertion and extraction procedure.

Rereading that last sentence, I realise it sounds like a double entendre, but I can assure you that is purely coincidental, honest!

As we strapped in, James cautioned me that we would assess the wind at the threshold of the runway, which made sense, especially given that this was my first flight in this type.

Choke on, mags on, master on, a shout of "CLEAR PROP!" and the Rotax 503 was spinning on the electric starter. After a couple of seconds, the reassuring buzz of a two-stroke engine filled my ears and I set idle power.

Eagerly, I thumbed the transmit button, "Rossall Traffic, Golf Mike Yankee Yankee Lima entering and back tracking runway 02".

James grinned "Bet you were practising that call all last night, mate?"

I have to admit, I had run it through my mind more than once on the drive up, even though, ironically, there was no one else on frequency when I made the call, so only James and I heard my exceptionally well-practised R/T transmission.

Pushing the oversized throttle lever forwards to apply a little of the power from the 50 stallions in the Rotax two-stroke stable that was bolted above my head, we began to taxy down the runway.

Turning as late as possible to ensure we had the maximum runway available to us, I lined up, a little off the centre line, which James promptly pointed out to me "around you go again mate". So, power on, right rudder and round we went, this time lining up much better.

Another check of the windsock confirmed the wind was still quite brisk but not dangerous, I glanced at James and raised my eyebrows – "We good?"

"Yes mate, let's go for it."

A quick check of the instruments to confirm the exhaust and cylinder head temps were in the green and I pushed the throttle forwards to the stop, whilst applying a little left rudder. A small smile began to light up my face and we started to accelerate. As we gathered speed down the runway, I felt every bump and imperfection as the volume of the Rotax soundtrack continued to increase. I focused on keeping the aircraft tracking straight, and continued the take-off, and then, after what felt like a surprisingly short ground run, and quite suddenly, the bumping stopped.

I was airborne for the first time in my own aeroplane…

But the story of this flight, and indeed of this aeroplane, starts a long time before this windy take-off in the North West of England in 2018. It starts back in the late 1970s, when I was just a boy.

This is the story of my Cyclone AX3/503, serial number 7110 – registration G-MYYL, to many just Yankee Lima, or as I have named her, 'Harriet' after my late Nan who inspired me to be all that I can be. It is a story of farsighted entrepreneurs and flying adventures; of novice mistakes and skilled instructors, and it is, of course, the story of the people who constantly look skywards: the pilots and owners of G-MYYL.

Yankee Lima's story is in many ways inseparable from the story of early microlighting as a whole, certainly three-axis microlights, and the transformation of these early machines from hang gliders with engines attached in the 1970s to the three-axis conventionally controlled flying machines that the public recognise as aeroplanes.

It Started with a Dream

I'd wanted to fly for as long as I can remember. Probably since before I could properly walk, and definitely before I could run (although I've since discovered I quite like this too). As a kid I was constantly looking skywards.

I used to watch the BBC TV programme "Reaching for the Skies" religiously every week, back when TV was scheduled and the concept of 'bingeing on a box set' had not even been thought of. I vividly remember being so moved that I would occasionally even become emotional watching it and declared to my mum - "Mum, I have to fly!" This was a good 30 years before I started crying at any film with a father/daughter separation scene in it. Yes, I'm afraid that does include Disney films too.

I read any book I could get my hands on that had a flying angle. I got suckered in to the weekly part works like 'Airplane' and even bought the matching binders which I still have proudly on my bookshelves, much to my wife's disdain.

I built plastic Airfix kits of model aircraft and I visited the Cosford air show. I played flight simulators that were running on the expansive computing power of my Sinclair ZX Spectrum 48k, and, when I was old enough, I joined the Air Cadets.

I once built a balsa glider directly from a set of free plans I received with a model aircraft magazine (yes, I bought those too). I carefully selected the wood from the local model shop and, with a great deal of patience I manufactured and assembled every single part and assembly. It took a while. Any part that didn't meet my quality criteria was discarded and recut.

It was a work of art when I had finally finished it and it was ready for that first flight.

It flew once.

This was when I launched it on a glide test flight from my parents' bedroom window into the garden below to test the flying characteristics. You see, although I couldn't afford the expensive radio gear or engine you needed to make it fly under its own steam, I did understand enough about weight and balance to position some ballast inside and get the centre of gravity correct.

Whilst in the Air Cadets (1444 Squadron) I was privileged to have my first flight in an aircraft of any kind (we didn't do holidays to Benidorm, so I'd never been on a jet or anything). So, whilst on camp at RAF Hereford I was taken for my first ever trip into the skies in an RAF Puma helicopter! Not only this, but the pilot took us flying round the Welsh mountains at low level with the doors open. I'd been waiting for this moment my whole life. So how did I celebrate? By throwing up copiously into the conveniently provided sick bags. I bet the pilot was pissing himself with laughter at me. I'll also wager he won that day's little game of "who can make the most cadets sick on Air Experience Flights?"

Anyway, despite this rather inauspicious start to my flying career, I was not put off. I went flying again later that year with the cadets, getting to take the controls of a Venture self-launching glider, and also at some point around this time my dad arranged for his mate to take me and my brother up in a Piper Cherokee flying from Sleap. My brother, Matt, graciously allowed me to sit in the front as he knew how much it meant to me. He would also be part of the story when I made my decision to learn to fly some 25 years later.

After leaving school and being rejected by the RAF on medical grounds, 'normal' life took over, I got a job and the dream of flying faded into the background. Don't get me wrong, I was still mad keen on anything with wings, but I didn't have the money or time to learn to fly. Well money really, and I'd discovered night clubs, and beer, and girls…

Then in my mid-thirties I joined the local gliding club and started to rekindle my passion for the skies. I was doing well and had been learning for around three months, but again real life had other ideas and I had to stop before I even got competent enough to go solo.

Finally, as I was approaching 40 and after my brother and his wife had brought me a flight simulator experience in a full flight Boeing 737 simulator, I approached my local microlight school about lessons. I finally had a little disposable income and it really wasn't as expensive as I'd thought it might be. Ten months later and I was shaking hands with the CFI who was congratulating me on passing my General Skills Test. I was a pilot at last!

However, despite having acquired the 'licence to learn', it would be another few years before I would be in a position to own my own aeroplane.

Birth of the Weedhopper

Having finally taken my own AX3 into the skies I was interested in finding out more about the machine which now has my late Nan's name adorning the cockpit. But where to start?

Well, like all good modern post millennial researchers, I reached for my laptop and typed www.google.com (other search engines are available) into the browser. And thus, began my investigation into the story of Yankee Lima, or to me, Harriet.

The origins of Yankee Lima, and indeed every Cyclone AX3, can be traced back to one of the earliest microlights – the Chotia Weedhopper – and to the American state of Utah and a company unsurprisingly called 'Weedhopper of Utah'. The company was created in the late 1970s to manufacture and distribute the Chotia Weedhopper JC24, a small single seat microlight designed by John Chotia [1]. This was in the very early days of microlighting, in fact, it was before the term had even been widely accepted; during the late 70s aircraft of this type were often simply referred to as powered hang gliders, or even, minimum aeroplanes. It was a period during which the pioneers of our sport were experimenting with new ideas and designs, and it was at this time that the word 'ultralight' began to be used. Sometime after this in the UK, we adopted the word microlight to refer to the same type of aircraft (as for some reason our island nation always has to be different) – but the rest of the world still uses 'ultralight' today.

I imagine this period was very much like a late 20th Century ultralight version of the very early days of aviation in the time of the Wright brothers.

In the USA, during this time, there was very little in the way of regulation of ultralights; in fact you did not even need a Pilot's licence to fly one. This lack of regulation encouraged entrepreneurial enthusiasts to create and build this new industry at an extremely fast pace. John Chotia was one such person. A former NASA engineer who had an interest in hang gliding, he'd seen a gap in the aviation market for a more affordable type of powered flying machine and had designed and built an aeroplane to fill it.

At the time, if you wanted to fly, you needed to get a pilot's licence and also either buy a share or rent a far more expensive general aviation machine like a Cessna 172 or Piper PA28. This cost was beyond the means of most American families, and Chotia understood this. He envisaged the JC-24 Weedhopper to fill this gap in the market as a machine that could be purchased, built in a garage from a premanufactured kit, assembled and flown by a single occupant without all the expensive regulation that comes with the oversight of the FAA or the need to have to complete expensive pilot training.

Many people had their doubts that this could succeed, but after a few early hiccups the result was the JC-24 Weedhopper (Chotia's 24th design, hence the name). By 1981, his company was doing well and attracted the interest of then Denver-based, New York Times reporter Bill Schmidt who wrote an article on the fledgling company entitled 'ULTRALIGHT PLANES: FLYING VERSION OF THE 5-CENT CIGAR' which was published in the New York Times in June 1981 [2].

Here was a well-respected and subsequently accomplished journalist who spent over 30 years at the NY Times. Turning to the internet once more and having found that Schmidt was now working as a university lecturer, I fired off a speculative e-mail to see if he could recall anything about his encounter with John Chotia some 37 years later.

Not being an aviation man himself, Schmidt had heard about Weedhopper and the novelty of it had piqued his interest. So, on his next trip to Utah he gave John Chotia a call and arrangements were made to visit the factory and find out more about the fledgling ultralight.

Unsurprisingly the intervening 37 years have meant that a lot of the details of that meeting have faded from Bill's memory, but he did remember the meeting itself and being amazed by the Weedhopper. Bill continues:

"I know little about flying and aircraft, but was attracted to the novelty of it – the idea you could build your own working aircraft from a kit....and actually fly. I recall being amazed by the Weedhopper itself – it looked so small and fragile, and sounded little a model airplane with its little buzzing engine. Mr. Chotia took one up for a spin, while I watched from the ground."

The Weedhopper was succeeding because of its simplicity. The control system was simple: a two-axis affair with elevator control for pitch and a rudder to control yaw and thus induce bank via the large Dacron covered wings with their large inbuilt dihedral angle. This system worked well and proved to allow untrained pilots to get to grips with flying the Weedhopper quite quickly. It was also not far removed from the 'normal' three-axis control systems of the larger GA aircraft.

19

Sadly, not long after this article was published, and just a few days before his thirty-fifth birthday, John Chotia was to die, test flying another of his own designs, the JC Rocket. However, his work has since been recognised by the Experimental Aircraft Association (EAA) who inducted Chotia into their Ultralight Hall of Fame in 2002 with the following citation:

"John Chotia: Chotia, who died in 1980, began building hang gliders in the 1960s and designed more than 30 full-size ultralight models, most notably the still-popular Weedhopper series. He also designed numerous aircraft parts and did early innovation on man-powered flight." [3]

New Engines and a New Name – Welcome the AX3

Researching the history of the Weedhopper and John Chotia whetted my appetite for further investigation into how this early simple machine became the AX3 I own today. One thing that really helped to improve the aeroplane was a better engine as the early engines proved to be quite underpowered.

Initially the early pre-production machines of the Weedhopper had been fitted with a 292cc Yamaha engine which cranked out a 'huge' 19HP at 5000RPM [1]. This was just about sufficient for a single seat machine - which still only had two-axis control - but Chotia was not a fan of the high rpm of the available snowmobile derived engines and wanted something less noisy.

The answer? Obvious really - he set about designing his own engine, you know, as you do, which he christened the Chotia 460. This delivered 18.5 hp at a much lower rpm of 3500 – similar to the speed at which more conventional light aircraft engines run. This in turn meant no need for a reduction gearbox (saving weight) and allowed him to fit a direct-drive propeller, again more akin to the Cessna and Piper world.

The Aircraft Engine Owner's manual described this new powerplant as:

"The Chotia (Cho-da)-460 is a unique two-cycle engine using battery ignition, super strong crank, mild timing, and manual advance ignition system." [4]

By fitting this engine Chotia had ensured that the weight of the Weedhopper would fall within the requirements of Federal Aviation Regulations (FAR) Part 103 ultralight aircraft.

The Weedhopper 2 had an improved version of the Chotia engine, and was eventually capable of producing 30HP but sadly, as was the case with a lot of early ultralight engines, was still quite unreliable. By 1983, the JC-24C with the Chotia 460D engine was the only model of the Weedhopper still being sold. And so, in order to take the Weedhopper to the next level in terms of both reliability and providing the performance required to accommodate the additional weight of a passenger, an alternative had to be found.

Although lots of success was achieved in marketing the JC24 in its single-seat form, room for a passenger would make flying much more fun. This is something I think we have all found as pilots over the years. Flying solo is great but sharing it with a friend or a member of your family makes it fabulous. It also makes duel instruction possible as well, something that has become accepted throughout most of the microlight world now.

Sadly, due to a combination of a poor reputation from the unreliable engines and also the lack of power, this was proving problematic to achieve.

Enter Rotax.

The now ubiquitous supplier of a large percentage of all ultralight engines in use today first enters the Weedhopper story with the introduction of the Rotax 277 which was used in the Weedhopper as standard. This engine produced around 28hp and was later replaced with the Rotax 447 with a massive 40hp that was installed in the confusingly named '40' model, as well as the Deluxe from around 1996 onwards [5].

The ultimate version of the Weedhopper was the Weedhopper 2 which featured side-by-side seating and the 50hp Rotax 503 engine.

However, this is where the story of the AX3 and Weedhopper diverge, although the Weedhopper continued to be produced for many years as a kit in the USA. After John Chotia's death, a Frenchman named Marc Mathot shifted production of the Weedhopper to France through his company, Ultralair. During 1985 a factory was completed and staff at Ultralair were trained on manufacturing the Weedhopper.

The design was then refined and improved with the addition of full three-axis controls alongside that second seat, a fully faired cockpit and Rotax 503 power.

The AX3 was born.

From the AX3 brochure: *"Featuring the renowned ROTAX engine, the CYCLONE AX3 is available with 3 engine options-on the mid-range 503 engine up to five hours' flying can be comfortably achieved with the aircraft's optional 50 litre fuel capacity."* [6]

Airbourne Aviation at Popham had an advert for the newly named Cyclone AX3 in the November/December 1992 edition of Microlight Flying Magazine that proclaimed: *"It's an absolute dream, and if it's good enough for the R.A.F to fly in on expedition to Gibraltar... well!"*

Things were looking very promising indeed for this new machine!

Buying G-MYYL, or How Do You Buy an Aeroplane Anyway?

So, back to mid-2017 and the question of how I came to end up with an AX3 as my aircraft of choice anyway?

I'd never really thought I would be able to own my own aircraft, and it wasn't really something that I had ever thought was achievable, certainly not whilst I had a mortgage etc. But it was an article in the July 2015 edition of Microlight Flying magazine that first planted the seed and put the AX3 onto my radar, enticingly entitled "Second-hand secrets", and promising me that I could get my own aeroplane for only a few thousand pounds. I was intrigued, and eagerly read more.

The photographs showed a microlight that looked like an aeroplane, with all the right bits in (roughly) all the right places. Engine at the front, tricycle undercarriage, wings above the cockpit, tail at the back and all flying surfaces of the conventional three-axis variety of ailerons, elevator and rudder.

The simplistic panel in the cockpit looked easy to understand and had its own charm too. Reading, and rereading the article I was more and more convinced that, yes, I could afford an aeroplane of my own.

G-MYYL's panel is simplicity itself!

Fast forward a couple of years and it'd been another frustrating month of Lancashire weather. I'd still not flown at the controls of an aeroplane for a couple of months.

I was bored, I was frustrated and I was fed up. So, I did the only logical thing that I could think of.

I bought an aeroplane.

It was mid-2017 and I'd been involved in an evening game of one of my favourite pastimes entitled "let's review every AX3 advert I can find on AFORS", a game I'm sure many pilots reading this will be familiar with. You probably have your own version of it that goes something like "let's review every <insert

desired aircraft type here> I can find on AFORS". For those of you that are unacquainted with AFORS, it is one of the main online sites for buying and selling all things aviation in the UK.

Eventually I clicked on the advert for an AX3 which promised the Rotax 503 engine had been overhauled only 20 hours ago and that everything worked "as it should" – it also ended with that characteristic car sales phrase "first to see will buy" [7]. However, in this case, it ended up being true!

I was a bit tired, I was a bit lonely, I had some other things on my mind and for whatever reason, decided to contact the owner and find out more about this aircraft.

After a few exchanged messages on Facebook, I went to bed and thought about the possibility of me actually buying an aeroplane. My mind was racing as I kept thinking, should I? Shouldn't I? Don't be ridiculous, and get a grip Dan…

And anyway, how do you even go about buying an aeroplane? It's not like buying a second-hand car and just going round and kicking the tyres with a gleeful yelp of – "How much for cash?"

With the benefit of hindsight, I now know that there is plenty of helpful advice to be found on the BMAA's website, including a buyers' guide. But when I started looking into this purchase, I had no idea where to start. In case you don't realise, the British Microlight Aircraft Association (BMAA) are the organisation that administer microlight flying within the UK on behalf of the Civil Aviation Authority.

So, I Googled, as you do, and after several hours 'research' and, realising that I knew less than zero about whether or not the wings would stay on, I decided to send round a BMAA inspector to check out the condition of Yankee Lima for me. A week or so later, the inspector duly went and checked over Yankee Lima and I eagerly anticipated his email report. This arrived a few days later.

"Unable to fly due to weather" stood out for me, but this was mitigated by the fact it had passed its annual permit inspection and check flight only a couple of months previously. It was kind of all academic anyway because in true Dan style I'd already decided I was going to buy her anyway, unless there was something catastrophically bad in the report.

I continued to scan to the bottom of the email.

"As said, for the age YL is in good condition. Still little things to do and a good clean."

This seemed like a satisfactory summary to my highly untrained eye. The next part of the e-mail contained the standard microlight pilots' warning that the engine may stop being an engine at any time and just become 30kg of useless ballast.

"Rotax two-strokes are not certified engines and could stop at any time; make sure you have a safe landing area in mind."

The narrative prompted a few questions from me which I quickly fired back, along with payment for the inspection and then thought of what to do next.

Logically I needed to go and see and fly the aeroplane. This was a seriously non-trivial logistical challenge as the aircraft was hangered in the south east of England, whereas I live in the North West, mostly.

However, at the time I was spending a lot of time in Holland, and at that moment, that is where I was.

Not to be put off, I fired up the Met Office app on my iPhone to be greeted by the standard pessimistic weather forecast offered up by their forecasting app. No problem. Smiling inwardly, I switched apps to one of the scores of alternative weather forecasting apps I have as a back-up until I found a suitable weather forecast that I liked. We all do that don't we?

It still wasn't great, but it looked like there might be a weather window. If I was lucky…

One quick phone call to the owner to square away the practicalities of where and when and then it was onto the more challenging part of this transaction.

How to convince my then girlfriend (now wife), Kaz and youngest daughter, Elektra, that what they really wanted and needed right now in their lives was a night away in a hotel on the edge of East Anglia and next to precisely nothing?

Actually, I'm doing them a disservice. It was a bit of a challenge with the timing of our holidays, but I wanted to see Yankee Lima before we went away and, hopefully, purchase her.

Like I said, I can be a bit impulsive, and had pretty much decided to make the purchase already, but felt I should go and do some due diligence, like kick the tyres or something. It kept my mum and Kaz happy (ish) anyway.

That day in late July 2017 went something like this.

We woke up in Den Haag, Holland and made our way to Schiphol airport for the early morning flight back to the UK. It's never nice to have to get up early but I needed every minute of the 24 hours available today if I was going to complete this logistical challenge successfully.

Landing back into Manchester Airport refreshingly on schedule, we collected my car from the long stay and began the trip down my favourite piece of transport infrastructure in the world.

The M6.

The road that for years now has taunted me with signs that say 50mph, while you are actually moving at something more akin to the walking pace of a dead sloth that's not in a rush to be anywhere.

Happily, on this occasion the road was functioning more in road mode, not the more prevalent car park mode, and we arrived in the Midlands to drop off my eldest daughter, Izzy, around midday as planned, before continuing down the length of the M6 to a place called Rockingham, home of the famous motor speedway, and as far as I could make out, bugger all else.

Bugger all else, that is, apart from the Hampton Inn, which was the nearest Hilton hotel to my intended destination of Priory Farm Airfield near Tibenham, Norfolk.

By the way, it's not that I am rich or anything: I had just accumulated a large number of Hilton points from work-related trips and that meant I could stay for free rather than pay a hotel bill! You know, we pilots don't like to pay for anything if we can get it for free.

So, with Kaz and Elektra checked in, and an afternoon of trampolining arranged at the handily located 'Gravity' trampoline park, equals happy child and happy Kaz, and by process of association, happy Dan. Happy Dan then jumped into the car and set course for Tibenham to see if he could become ecstatic aeroplane-owning Dan. As an added bonus, the weather was looking a little better than 50/50 as well.

Sorry, I'll stop referring to myself in the third person now.

I'd arranged to meet the aircraft's current owner, Tom, at around four o'clock that afternoon, with the intention of flying, weather permitting, and checking the aircraft over as best I could - kicking the tyres. As I arrived, the hurricane force winds that had battered the South East for most of the day were just dropping and there was even some blue sky around (yes, in England!).

I took this as a positive omen and Tom and I sauntered over to the hangar to view Yankee Lima whilst I nervously glanced at the windsock every few minutes. It was a hell of a long way to come and not fly…

Priory Farm Airfield is a lovely little farm strip nestled in East Anglia's flat and green farming countryside. It's right in the heart of where there are many former wartime RAF stations, including former RAF Tibenham right next door which has its own interesting history, both wartime and post war.

My favourite post-war story about RAF Tibenham is that the old control tower was allegedly haunted. And, I don't know how true this is; apparently some of the members of the gliding club based there would not enter the tower, even in daylight. There had been reports of a person being seen in flying clothes, similar to those worn by the USAAF wandering around darkened rooms. The old tower was demolished in the late Seventies, but Tibenham still has a very active gliding club based there today.

Now having done most of my flying from Barton's long grass runways, Priory Farm was something new to me: a very short grass strip with no ATS unit or anyone manning the radio. This was going to be an interesting new experience for me.

Another nervous glance at the windsock. Still OK.

Pulling Yankee Lima out of the gloom of the hangar, which was filled with an array of interesting aircraft types including a Cessna 120, Boeing Stearman biplane, Tipsy Nipper and an array of microlights, I stood back and appraised my aircraft-to-be.

And then we did the walk around. Tyre kicking time!

The nice thing about the AX3 is that as it is a simple aircraft you can see everything, including the control cables/rods and all the connections to the flying surfaces. The engine is clearly visible and conveniently mounted at head height for inspection. Everything seemed OK to my untrained, non-engineer's eye and the wind was still good.

So, we went flying.

Was she smooth, comfortable, quiet, relaxing to fly?

No.

No, she wasn't.

She was none of these things.

She was feisty and had an attitude, a bit like my Nan actually. And that's why I decided to name Yankee Lima 'Harriet', as I mentioned earlier.

The engine was smooth, don't get me wrong, but it was proper back to basics flying, I could feel the wind in the cockpit (plenty of manual air conditioning, as my Dad would say), it was loud and a lot lighter than other types I had flown and therefore I felt every gust of wind.

But.

Even though she was completely different to anything I had flown in before, and many other reasons, she was still perfect and I was hooked. The 45-50 mph cruise speed meant I had a lot of time to look around and enjoy the scenery. Everything happened a lot slower, and, when we landed, we stopped in about 10 feet! All right not quite 10 feet, but 60-70 metres.

As Tom turned the key to kill the mags and we rolled to a stop adjacent to the clubhouse, I hopped out and thought, this is what I want. I want to own my own plane with all the trouble, expense and hassle it brings, because it also brings a freedom that I had dreamed of since I was a small boy. I had visualised a day like this, well not quite like this, not starting in one country and then crossing half of another by a notoriously traffic filled motorway to stay in a hotel in the middle of nowhere and then fly one, windy circuit, from the passenger seat!

The day I dreamed of was turning up at the airfield at my convenience and going for a flight, before coming back to sit in the clubhouse and talk aviation over a cup of tea and a hobnob (well the gluten-free equivalent), and then maybe just hopping in and going off somewhere else, ideally with some clubmates.

That day was quite a way off yet, though.

Over a cup of tea in the clubhouse I looked through the logbooks and paperwork, trying with my incredibly untrained eye to look for anything out of the ordinary whilst desperately hoping not to find anything at the same time.

Finally (having already made up my mind) I said: "Tom, come outside and show me all the little things you would do if you kept her."

And there I was: an aircraft owner. Well, almost.

But that was only the beginning. I still had a long list of things to sort out including hangarage/parking at an airfield within an hour of my home and then the transportation of Yankee Lima back to the North West.

I'd been looking around for some time, for somewhere to base my aircraft. There were several sites to consider within my self-imposed one-hour drive time limitation: Carr Valley, St Michael's, Huddersfield, obviously Barton and Rossall Field. After a few phone calls and e-mails this was reduced to a choice between St Michael's and Rossall Field as Barton was too expensive, Huddersfield had no space and Carr Valley could only offer tie down space outside. And as inexperienced at aircraft ownership as I was, I reckoned keeping a 200kg microlight outside in the North West would quickly mean no microlight after the winter storms…

Rossall Field had space in the hangars and the rates were good, so I arranged to meet up with James. After a short tour of the hangars and a chat over a brew I decided there and then that this was to be the home for Yankee Lima.

But how to get her to her new home?

After much thought, and advice, I decided to hire a specialist aircraft ferry firm to move Yankee Lima by road. I had originally intended to fly back myself, but with zero time on type, no decent weather guarantee plus unfamiliar airspace to navigate, I decided that road haulage would be the sensible option (see Mum I can be sensible!).

After that I had to arrange insurance, something I'd not really considered before. After a little research I decided that given the purchase price of Yankee Lima, and also the cost of comprehensive insurance, termed hull insurance in aeronautical language, I would go the third party and passenger liability route. After looking around at a couple of websites I found this to be an unexpectedly pleasant and easy experience.

Fill in the handy online form.

Email it in.

Get an insurance policy in your inbox!

Awesome. This is how life should be - although I did note my new policy had a few disappointing exceptions as I read the terms and conditions:

"Your policy will not cover you for bodily injury and/or property damage sustained by the pilot in command of your aircraft"

Ok so I'm not covered if I hurt myself, no problem. But there was more...

"Your policy will not cover you for any hostile detonation of any weapon of war employing atomic or nuclear fission and/or fusion or other like reaction or radioactive force or matter."

Not really an issue, I suppose, but it got me wondering how many microlights are capable of carrying a nuclear weapon? This then led to me considering, and if you were carrying a nuclear 'weapon of war' and intended to use it, why on earth would you try and get insurance for it? On the plus side, I noticed it does not exclude the use of conventional air to air missiles, so I guess it's game on next time I've got an RAF Typhoon in my sights….

Either way, I presume that Kim Jong-un uses a different insurer for his nuclear bomber microlight fleet.

With my freshly minted insurance policy in my pocket, well inbox, I also needed to consider how I would assemble my new aeroplane after transport by road 'oop north', but there's a whole chapter on my experience of this later in this book.

I needed to purchase a radio, intercom and other bits of kit, but you know what? I'm a boy. And I like kit. Especially kit that is electrical. The kind of presents you would have been delighted to have as a kid at Christmas instead of the soft woollen package of doom, containing something vaguely soft and knitted by Aunt Mabel and styled by Stalin's "Ministry of Clothing".

Finally, I figured I should have some conversion onto type training. Whilst not needed legally, Yankee Lima was a different animal to anything I had flown previously, so I thought it would be prudent to take an instructor up with me first, to get the hang of the different flying characteristics.

I was soon to discover just how easy it is to spend money on anything flying related. This resolved my 'kit' problems, and a quick chat with James confirmed that he would happily fly with me. Sorted.

Interest from the Royal Air Force and "Military" Service

One night during one of my 'I want to know everything there is to know about the AX3' moments, other people probably just call this research; I came across a photograph of an AX3 in RAF colours! This surprised me, as I'm sure it does you, as I had never heard of the RAF using microlights for air defence activities, although I have intercepted both a Lancaster bomber and an RAF Typhoon in microlight aircraft, more on this later.

Back to that photograph, which is reproduced further on, and I decided to initiate a few threads on popular flying forums Pprune and Microlight Forum to see if I could discover the story behind the photograph. Astonishingly, my research revealed that an unlikely marriage between the RAF and the AX3 very nearly happened.

It was during the early 1990s that this interesting anecdote from the AX3's history occurred. The RAF's Air Experience Flight (AEF) were looking for suitable aircraft to replace the fleet of Chipmunks that had served to provide ear-to-ear grinning for Air Cadets for almost a generation. The obvious cost savings that a cheap microlight aircraft could offer, not only in maintenance, but in purchase costs meant that some senior officers in the RAF could see the benefit in having a larger fleet of these more cost-effective aircraft.

One pilot who was involved in this evaluation was Terry Clark. He was an instructor at 2409 squadron at the time, and takes up the story:

"In the early '90s, the use of microlights for flying cadets was 'officially' frowned upon and squadrons were told that 'microlight flying was not an approved Air Cadet activity', however, to HQ Air Cadets, microlights were of the weight shift variety and those in charge were unwilling to accept the rate of development of other designs.

As more 'robust' designs were developed with 'normal' 3 -axis controls, the OC of No 2409 (RAF Halton) Sqdn ATC got the manufacturers of the original Thruster to 'lend' him one with a promise he would make every effort to 'sell' the concept to HQ Air Cadets.

I had a PPL but due to official policy, I kept the operation at arm's length rather than leap in and get involved.

Then in May 1991, a letter went out to squadrons in Herts and Bucks Wing ATC inviting any adult staff with PPLs who might be interested to come along to a 'look/see' day at Halton to find out what microlights were about and have a free ride in one.

Not being one to turn down a free flight, although I was a bit dubious about how safe microlights were, I went along on the specified date, 26 May 1991. I arrived to find the Thruster parked outside the microlight operator's caravan, alongside another microlight of an unfamiliar design with a strange registration. This yellow painted aircraft had a nosewheel undercarriage rather than the tailwheel of the Thruster.

Within minutes, I was introduced to Bill Sherlock of Cyclone Airsports, who took me over to this 'other' aircraft which he called the AX3, its 'strange' registration (F59EE) being apparently French Class 'B' markings indicating it was a prototype or experimental aircraft.

We strapped in, Bill pointing out that although lightweight in construction, it was made of triangular tubular sections making it very robust.

Anyway, we started up and Bill taxied us out to the take-off point. He did the first take-off, talking me through it and handed over to me once we were airborne.

I climbed to 1,000ft QFE, quite a good rate of climb, flying a 'normal' circuit pattern left hand on runway 02 (I was already familiar with Halton having been associated with 613 Gliding School for many years including being an Air Cadet Glider pilot cleared for air experience flying) and with the occasional advice from Bill, flew an approach and landed, to which Bill said 'well done, greaser first time'. He then suggested we taxy back and I tried a take-off which once again was quite straight forward.

We flew another circuit then taxied back in to allow the next 'volunteer' a go.

I was hooked!"

As the aircraft was not designed for flying with Air Cadets in mind, several changes were recommended in order to make it more palatable to the powers that be. Terry recalls:

"As Halton is an RAF station, the OC airfield had to be involved with the operation. OC airfield (not the Station Commander)

40

was in these days an experienced RAF pilot of Squadron Leader rank and he was very keen on the microlight operation so he carried out the initial evaluation of the AX3 and made two main recommendations:

1. *The aircraft as presented had two instrument panels: one above the windscreen with engine instruments and another below the windscreen with flight instruments. These needed to be grouped into a single panel below the windscreen.*

2. *There was no floor so nowhere for the pilot not flying to rest their feet.*

This was communicated to Ultralair by Bill and they readily agreed to carry out these mods, so Bill and Rob (OC Halton Squadron ATC) paid several visits to the CAA to get UK approvals arranged and a registration allocated. Ultralair asked what colour scheme was required so they were sent a photo of a Tucano in the standard colour scheme of red and white.

Sometime later, those of us who had attended the initial evaluation day were invited back because representatives of HQ Air Cadets were coming along to 'check out' the suitability of the AX3 in its refined version for cadet flying."

In fact, that colour scheme of an RAF training aircraft ended up being recreated a little too accurately on the first aircraft delivered to the Ridge Runners and included roundels on the wings and fin flashes! I bet the cadets would have loved to fly in that; it looked just like an RAF trainer in that scheme.

G-MYER looking rather dashing in RAF Training Command colours

Graeme Park was building hours north of the border at Oban in early 1991. He was starting to look around for a training aircraft that was easier for the student to fly than the Thruster and also more comfortable for the instructor than the Shadow, which was a very quick microlight.

"I first flew the AX3 Premier, registered F-59EE with Jon George at Popham on 18/3/91. Mac Smith's school there was also looking at replacing Thrusters with the AX3, which it subsequently did. I later flew the Cyclone AX3, registered F-59GD with Bill Sherlock, the UK importer at Drayton St. Leonards on 8/7/91."

Graeme went on to obtain his AFI rating (the first step on the instructor ladder) and subsequently pass the FI exam the following year. Shortly after that he picked up his own AX3, G-MYHG, and trailered it up to Scotland where he performed his first flight from Strathaven Airfield in late January 1993. Being the Scottish agent for AX3 distribution, Graeme demonstrated HG at many airfields in the Scotland and the north of England including East Fortune and Eshott amongst others.

Graeme Park's G-MYHG

However, the AX3, in its initial form had limited cross-country capability without refuelling.

Graeme continues: *"Since it only had one 24 litre fuel tank, it was severely limited in range (just over two hours @ 45-50mph airspeed) but was a great wee trainer, albeit with a rather fragile nosewheel, and could get in (and out of) the smallest fields imaginable. I did not sell any in Scotland, although a few subsequently appeared. but I did over 500 hours in G-MYHG. The only other AX3 I flew was G-MYER, which had a 582 and two fuel tanks.*

It was subsequently called an AX-2000. This machine was loaned by Bill Sherlock to Hugh Knox who flew it from Central Scotland to Shetland and then for five hours across the sea to Norway [he must have had a bloody tailwind!] *in formation with Tom Grieve in a weight-shift microlight in Summer 1994, I think. This was to commemorate the first flight across the North Sea on July 30, 1914 by Tryggve Gran who flew the 510 km (320 mi) from Cruden Bay in Scotland to Jæren in Norway in 4 hours and 10 minutes. Hugh and Tom then flew across the Skagerrak to Denmark, through Holland and Belgium then across the Channel to England. The icing on the cake was flying across the Irish Sea to Ireland then back to Stonehouse in Scotland!"*

"As far as I am aware, at least initially, all UK-registered AX3s were built at the Drayton St Leonard 'factory'- actually a tarted-up farm shed. I never heard Bill talk about flying the demonstrators across the Channel so assume they were built in France and trailed over derigged, exactly how I later got my own AX3 from Drayton St Leonard to Scotland. Unlike the Kitfox etc, it was not a quick derig/rig but it was doable."

I was to discover quite soon just how 'easy' to rig the AX3 was. But more on that later…

Terry:

"I remember F59GD; it was a much-improved version having larger wheels and a Rotax 582 engine. Bill lent it to the Halton operation (by now named the 'Ridge Runners') for a couple of weeks but I never got to fly it as the weather was too bad for a while.

Anyway, the upshot of the visit from HQ Air Cadets (thinking back now I believe one of them was actually from CFS) was that although the aircraft flew well, they were unable to commit public funds to support us due to the Rotax engines not being certified aircraft engines. We were allowed to fly cadets provided their parents gave consent via a special 'blood chit' which was derived from a template contained in AP1919 however so the cadets could record the flights in their logbooks."

But despite the reticence of the RAF, Terry also recalls:

"It handled crosswinds very well compared to some aircraft.

One day at Halton, we were getting 310/20kt gusting 25 - 28 so I taxied out to runway 28. This grass runway was quite wide so I lined up diagonally so I could take-off pretty much into wind - I'd had a 'moment' on an earlier flight when one wing lifted prematurely due to a gust, so I gently started opening the throttle and thought 'this is smoother than I expected'. The reason for this was that I was already airborne in about 50ft on just over half throttle so I opened up fully and climbed away!"

Air Vice-Marshal Merriman, the former head of the Empire Test Pilot School, test flew several microlights, the AX3 amongst them, to evaluate them for the AEF. The flights were carried out using 59GD, which was then registered G-MYER and given pre-approval CAA exemption to allow demonstration flights.

Air Commodore Colville was Stationed at RAF Alconbury, and was a huge fan of microlights for RAF cadet air experience flying. He borrowed G-MYER from Bill Sherlock for a couple of weeks and took it to Alconbury. It was during that period that Bill received a phone call that went along the lines of:

"I am Squadron Leader XYZ from RAF Alconbury. Are you the owner of microlight aircraft G-MYER?"

"Yes" replied Bill.

"Good, *then can you explain to me what your noisy little aeroplane is doing illegally performing aerobatics in my airspace at RAF Alconbury!"*

To which Bill calmly answered: *"I am not really sure, you will have to ask your Station Commander – Air Commodore Colville, who has the aircraft on loan!"*

A very fumbled and embarrassed sign off to the call followed.

The AX3 did well during the evaluation, impressing the RAF with its side-by-side seating, lower drag than many contenders and tricycle undercarriage layout with nose wheel steering. There were criticisms, of course, but this 'feedback' was addressed in short order by Ultralair as described earlier. Following this, a plan was soon devised by RAF Support Command to take a pair of AX3s on an epic journey to Barcelona to really put them through their paces and complete a more thorough assessment [8].

Sadly, changing priorities and a revised training programme meant that the Scottish Aviation Bulldog ended up being the aircraft selected for the AEF, and the RAF ditched their microlight-based plans. That said, the RAF Microlight Association at Halton did use several AX3s for training for many years.

Despite all of this, the dalliance with the RAF did give Bill Sherlock of Cyclone Airsports the impetus to refine the design and incorporate the improvements needed to meet the CAA's exacting Section S requirements for factory approval.

How to Assemble an Aeroplane

Bringing the story back to the present day and I was watching intently as the trailer was reversed in a rather haphazard manner towards the hangar. It was late in the day and the driver was over an hour and a half later than anticipated.

"Whoa," I warned as, whilst playing amateur banksman, I was very nearly embedded between the corner of the now stationary trailer and the row of metal shipping containers lining the wall to my right. Luckily the driver must have heard my yelp and belatedly eased the reversing trailer to a halt.

James and I looked at each other as we waited. The driver hopped down - well he didn't exactly hop as he wasn't exactly in the first flush of youth, but either way eventually made his way towards us.

Lowering the ramp, I anxiously scanned the contents of the trailer to ensure that everything looked ok. I could see the fuselage, two wings, the tail and assorted tubes and struts. OK quick count over, there were two of everything that there should be, the main fuselage and it had an engine.

OK so far.

As he nonchalantly started to unload my new aircraft "kit", pieces were passed to me in a rather confident manner. I handled these pieces of fabric and aluminium like a new born baby. Like they would break if I were to mishandle them in the slightest way. I've not felt so unskilled or ill prepared for anything since the birth of my first daughter.

As I held the newly acquired tail components of Harriet, questions raced through my mind:

"How do I hold it?"

"Where do I put it?"

"Can I just lean it on the wall? Or will that damage it?"

"Do I need to rest it on something?"

Excited and ambitious thoughts of a new title such as "Dan the Aircraft Engineer" were now far from my mind. I was out of my depth and I was quickly starting to realise it.

Fortunately, James (the CFI at Attitude Airsports, my new home base) was on hand to help me unload all the parts and offer advice on the best way to store my derigged microlight until such time as I could assemble her.

So, parts unloaded and safely laid out in the hangar, documents and keys received, I paid the driver and he set off on his long journey back to the south of England. At this point I was really glad I had chosen to employ the services of a professional aircraft ferry company, rather than hire a box van and do the journey myself, as I had been considering.

As mentioned earlier, I had originally been considering flying the aircraft up myself. But after a bit of thought and advice, I decided against this particular "adventure" which had a high degree of probability that I would end up an unwitting movie star on the next episode of 'Air Crash Investigations'.

After having a good look around and ensuring all the parts were secure, I left Harriet tucked up in her new hangar, in pieces.

The biggest aeroplane kit I've ever set eyes on!

It would be over three weeks before I set eyes on her again due to previously booked holiday/work commitments.

This was torture.

I owned my own plane and I couldn't get there to play with her!!

It was three weeks later and I'd just arrived home. The preceding weeks had consisted of around 10 days in Holland for work, nearly a week in Greece to visit my parents and then a week's family holiday in the north of England. During this time, predictably, the UK had some of the best flying weather that we had seen that year…

Also, during this time, I had constantly been thinking about visiting the airfield and starting work on Harriet.

Well today was the day. I was up early, kissed Kaz on the cheek and, after packing the car with all the paraphernalia one needs to maintain an aircraft, set off with the smell of coffee filling my nostrils from the travel cup I had hastily filled.

It was time to go to work.

I had originally envisioned assembling Harriet with some expert help from someone who actually knew how to rig a microlight. This was probably due in part to my total lack of knowledge in this area. So, for this initial visit, I intended to do some cleaning of the airframe, and any work that was easy for a layperson to do. My rationale was that it is easier to get in and clean an aircraft when it is already in bits.

So that initial day I spent tentatively pulling back the Ultralam fabric and identifying what I could and couldn't clean. Photographing everything obsessively before I disassembled anything in order to ensure that I could reassemble it correctly after cleaning.

It was a very enjoyable day, and I relished just being around the airfield, cleaning my aircraft, getting to know where everything in the fuselage was, and also identifying some simple parts that were either missing or unserviceable that could easily be purchased from B&Q and replaced.

Wow, was it really going to be that easy? I was really pleased with myself by the end of the day. To the untrained eye, I'd not really achieved much. But I had cleaned the entire rear portion of the fuselage both inside and out, I'd replaced some pipe insulation that is used to stress the fuselage skin, and also started to replace a lot of missing or broken cable ties. I'd also identified that the para cord ties were completely unserviceable and would fail soon, so I replaced those as well.

Not a bad first day in my new role as an apprentice aircraft engineer, I mused as I walked happily to my car amidst the lengthening shadows cast by the setting sun.

A week later I returned with some not-so-hired help in the form of my eldest daughter, Isobel. She was 13 back then and didn't quite share my enthusiasm for flying, but she does sometimes enjoy herself, or at least that's what I like to tell myself.

Earlier that weekend, casually over breakfast when asked "what are we doing tomorrow Dad?" I'd replied "Oh, we'll probably go up to the airfield and see if we can build an aeroplane."

I think she must be good at facial expressions, or else she genuinely was interested, as she exclaimed: "Oh good, I can't wait," accompanied by a huge injection of enthusiasm into her teenage voice.

We arrived at the airfield mid-morning and she helped me carry my "aircraft boxes" into the hanger. These were the tools, lubricants and other associated 'stuff' that I was fast realising are essential to any aircraft owner. After she had placed them down, she surveyed the pieces of (what I assured her was) an aircraft with a look of bewilderment on her face.

Quizzically she asked: "What do we do first Dad?"

"That is a damned good question," I mused.

I mean, here we were, faced with this pile of tubes, Ultralam, an engine, and a collection of bolts. Oh, and a I had a dogeared pilot's operating handbook which had a section I enthusiastically turned to, deceptively entitled as follows

"Rigging"

Ah, good, I thought, there are instructions. I read on with relish.

"To rig the aircraft simply reverse the above steps"

Oh.

To make matters worse, this was underneath the section that only described partial derigging, not removing the tail and rudder assembly for long distance transport, as had been the case for Harriet's journey.

Not to worry, I flicked to the long-distance derigging section and my eyes scanned to the bottom to locate the section marked "Rigging".

There wasn't one.

Just a reassuring paragraph that stated

"Warning"

"Microlights normally wear out faster from rigging, derigging and transit than they do from flying."

Okaaay.

So, assembly of Harriet was going to be a challenge. But then I reasoned to myself, I've done 1000-piece jigsaw puzzles before without instructions. How hard can it be?

However, somewhere else in the manual it did mention how the aircraft can be rigged or derigged by one person in around one to two hours. Ok, so that shouldn't be too hard then. More on this statement later…

Anyway before we got to the exciting part of working out which bits of metal tube went where (important), which way round the trim tab controls should be connected (quite important) and which way round to connect the aileron control cables (very important), and how to attach the wings so that they, erm, stay attached (extremely important), we still had some cleaning to do.

Isobel threw herself into this task with an amazing amount of verve and enthusiasm for someone who doesn't really seem that interested in mechanical engineering, or aircraft, or anything really that doesn't say twenty one pilots, Fall Out Boy or Panic! At the Disco on it. For my older readers i.e. anyone over the age of about 20, these are all bands whose brand of music is described as "alternative". As it happens, I quite like some of the music she plays, so we do have some things in common after all.

She particularly enjoyed playing with the hosepipe to wash down the cockpit and also cleaning the wings. After this she was asking: "What can I do now Dad?" So, I tasked her with replacing the 'draught proof' strips on the top of the door frames.

I've put that in quotes because, with the benefit of hindsight and experience flying Yankee Lima, she is anything but draught proof.

AX3s all come as standard fitted with what my father would have described in his career as a car sales executive as "copious manual air conditioning", or in less obfuscated language, holes.

Lots of holes!

Anyway, the strips were duly replaced and after figuring out how to reseat the doors on the hinge correctly, they do actually, almost seal, kind of, at the top anyway (is that enough mitigation for you?).

Next up, we spent some time polishing the lexan windscreen and doors, which revealed that one of my long-term tasks would be to replace these as it was quite badly scratched in places.

I took out my now lengthening notebook of jobs and added it to the list.

As we approached the middle of the afternoon on this third day, I was starting to think about putting bits of aircraft together, instead of leaving them on the hangar floor again for another week. I think subconsciously I had been putting this bit off because really, I had no idea what I was doing and, as mentioned above, the handbook was less than intuitive when it came to the section on assembling the aircraft.

Still, and I can't remember quite how I came to the decision, I reasoned that as I am the one who is going to be flying Harriet, who better to put her together? I'd rather trust my own work than someone else in this situation. Let's face it, I have far more invested in the aircraft staying in one piece as I apply the throttle to full than someone who is sitting on the ground supping a nice cup of tea watching me hurtle down the runway as bits of wing fall off!

So, when Izzy turned to me with a questioning expression upon her face for the umpteenth time that day and said: "Dad, what do you want me to do next?"

"Fetch the tail and let's see if we can start making these bits of plane into an aircraft, shall we?" was my reply.

"Cool!!" was the excited reply I received, along with a beaming smile as she skipped into the hangar to retrieve the tail assembly.

I reached down and picked up the battered manual and tried to find the section describing removal of the tail assembly and tried to rework it into reverse in my head. Not easy…

To make this quite challenging task (to someone who has never assembled a microlight before) even more confusing, I also had a bag of bolts/fasteners and nuts that I had to try and fathom from which to choose to bolt the tail to the rear part of the fuselage.

After selecting what looked like the appropriate bolts and nuts from the dark oily bag, I gave them a bit of a clean with some degreaser. Next, I rustled through my sports direct bag - you know the huge £1 ones they always try and flog you when you go in to buy a pair of socks, looking for a spanner, but was unsuccessful in this quest.

WARNING – please stop reading now if you are at all offended by the use of inappropriate tools for the job.

After a bit more hunting, I gleefully pulled out... a pair of pliers.

I know, I know. Please don't judge me, but I was keen to get on with assembling Harriet and figured they would be ok for the job.

That is, I did until James walked across the hangar and with a look of abject horror on his face said: "What are you doing? You heathen!"

Fair point...

He offered me the use of his tools until such time as I could acquire a more appropriate set for the task, which I gladly accepted.

Anyway, I lined up the tail with the appropriate holes and they all matched. Bingo! With a bit of assistance from James I managed to attach everything and then stood back to admire my work.

Oops.

I'd got the washers on the wrong side. i.e. they were doing nothing.

So, horizontal stabiliser off again, adjust position of said washers, and, off we went again.

Once the tail was rigged and the vertical stabiliser in place (this was considerably easier). It was time to figure out how to connect all the cables and control rods to the control surfaces.

Ideally in a manner that means the aircraft is actually capable of controlled flight, and not just looking like an aeroplane…

This actually turned out to be quite straightforward too. The rudder cable connections are described in quite some detail in the Pilot's Operating Handbook, and they emphasise all the important points (like ensuring they are crossed) so that it's difficult to make a mistake.

The elevator control rod was also quite easy to fathom. Less obvious was how the trim tab controls attached, but fortunately because the Ultralam covering is quite old (I presume it is original), there was a nice trim tab control cable plate shaped mark to line it up with on the elevator.

This pleased me.

A lot!

And that was enough for that day. Time was running out and we needed to get home so we put Harriet to bed and packed away our stuff and headed home.

She was starting to look like an aircraft, though…

Fast forward three days and, after traversing the southern Pennines, we were greeted by a beautiful day at Rossall Field, albeit slightly damp underfoot. This time I had the help of two of my daughters to assist with the big day of "putting the wings on".

Also, I secretly hoped we could start the engine as well, but I kept that to myself (well myself and the internet via Facebook AKA The Whole World).

Elektra and Izzy busied themselves unloading the tools – yes, I had now acquired a suitable toolkit containing pretty much everything I needed to treat Harriet with dignity and respect. Or put another way, not mash up every nut/screw and bolt with a pair of pliers as I didn't have the appropriate tools! Jeremy Clarkson eat your heart out!

We pulled Harriet out into the shade of the hangar (and wind) and positioned her so we could start to rig the wings.

I'll confess I'd been quite nervous about this bit, as obviously the wings are the most important part of an aircraft. In fact, they are what put the air, in aircraft. Otherwise it would just be a 'craft', and not a very good one at that.

It's vital they are attached correctly and securely, as per the design, and, well, the POH just wasn't very good at explaining how to do this:

"The aircraft can be rigged or derigged by one person in around one to two hours."

I've actually read better flat pack furniture instructions before, and we all know how they end up...

It's generally a given that you have not assembled it correctly unless you have bits left over after a self-assembly project. Ask Ikea.

However, with a bit of care and attention to detail between the three of us, and with some assistance from some of the other Rossall-based pilots, and literally zero help from the POH, we gradually turned Harriet into an aeroplane again.

The assembly itself consisted of selecting the correct lift strut, orienting it the correct way, lining it up on the slots and then inserting some chunky metal pins to hold it in place. These pins, in turn are then secured with the appropriately named "safety rings". Called so as they are there to prevent the pins falling out, and then the, erm, wing falling off the aeroplane at an inconvenient time, like when you are in the sky, for example...

Next, we had to connect the aileron controls and the pitot tube.

The pitot tube turned out to be quite straightforward: simply push all the bits of pipe together. For non-pilots – the pitot tube points directly into the airflow and is used by the airspeed indicator to measure airspeed. If it is blocked or incorrectly connected, the pilot will not have any indication of their airspeed on the ASI and will have to fly the aircraft based on the view out of the window (you should do this anyway!), the feel of the flight controls and the noise/draught in the cockpit.

The ailerons however, turned out to be more of a faff. They are controlled by two main control cables and a linked return cable, all connected to a set of span-length torque tubes. Connecting the main control cables was easy enough; these are the ones that make the aileron move up when you move the control column in the correct sense. But in order to make it move down in the opposite direction to the other aileron the return cable needs to be linked to the aileron torque tube via a pulley at the back of the fuselage which is in an extremely inaccessible place.

It's right at the back, you cannot get to it from the outside, and getting to it from the inside is tricky as you can't just lean on the skin of the aircraft. It's made of Ultralam and not designed to bear the weight of a normal human man.

Sorry that was a reference to The Fast Show (you either know or you don't), I can't help myself sometimes.

At this point the phrase "the aircraft can be rigged or derigged by one person in around one to two hours" flashed through my mind as I tried to contort myself in such a way as to connect the damn cable.

After much shouting, a small amount of swearing, a large dollop of frustration and a few gallons of tea, I finally managed to loop the cable around the pulley and connect it to the two aileron torque tubes:

"The aircraft can be rigged or derigged by one person in around one to two hours." - it actually took me well over an hour just to connect the aileron return cable.

But anyway, after all our hard work, here she is!

A fully rigged Harriet

She actually took around six to eight hours for us to rig, but it was our first time and I had not been involved in derigging her for the journey north so was having to figure things out as I went along.

The next job was to see if she would start.

Izzy and I manoeuvred Harriet out of the shadow of the hangar and pointed her into wind. Izzy then chocked the wheels and positioned herself with a camera to video the big event.

I climbed aboard and went through the pre-start checks.

Safe location ☑

Strapped in and hatches secure ☑

Throttle idle ☑

Brakes on ☑ (that's a laugh, brakes?)

Fuel system primed ☑

Choke full ☑ (more on this later)

All Clear ☑

Magnetos on, master on ☑

Shout "Clear prop!"

And I turned the starter key.

The prop spun making the staccato half choking noise that internal combustion engines make when trying to start on an electric starter motor.

Nothing.

I tried again:

"Clear prop!"

This time I got the half cough, splutter that your 1982 Ford Fiesta used to make in the depths of winter when it was "trying to start" and almost firing on one cylinder.

Hmm – this wasn't how it was supposed to happen.

I went through the checks again in my head. Had I missed something?

James came over and emptied the carb bowls and we tried again. Still nothing.

This was puzzling as when I had bought the aircraft, she had started first time, no problem and that was only about six weeks previously.

At this point though we had to call it a day, so reluctantly we wheeled Harriet back into her hangar spot and left with mixed feelings.

On the one hand, she looked like an aeroplane now, but currently she was nothing more than a glider if she wouldn't start.

Still Izzy did manage to capture a great picture of me performing my pre-start checks.

Trying to start Harriet for the first time

It was a week or so later when we finally got Harriet to fire. I'd been up a couple of times since and cleaned the spark plugs and replaced some missing split pins/safety rings (nothing to do with the engine not starting I hasten to add). I'd also tensioned the wing skins ready for flight. And eventually one Sunday morning James found the problem.

The problem was the idiot in the pilot's seat. Or as we often say in the world of IT, a PICNIC problem. Problem In Chair Not In Computer.

I had not been setting the choke fully open.

As simple as that.

Nothing wrong with the engine, nothing wrong with the ignition system or fuel system.

Just simple pilot error. The choke on the AX3 is a lever on the upper part of the cockpit. I had been turning it 90 degrees, assuming this was full on (like you would a fuel tap), but actually you had to move it almost 180 degrees and back on itself.

When you did this – she fired every single time. Which is reassuring when you are a pilot. The last thing you want is a temperamental engine.

So, with the engine running I performed some taxi checks – tested that the brakes would hold with at least 3000RPM (they held up to 4000) and got used to the ground handling.

At this point I guess you expect that I would describe lining up and going for that first flight. But alas, that story must wait for another chapter, as the British winter had already intervened and that was the last time Harriet would run until the New Year.

Approval? You Bet!

Returning back to the earlier days of the AX3, the aircraft was seen as a machine with lots of promise. Late in 1990, Keith Duckworth, of Cosworth fame, lent Bill Sherlock from Cyclone Airsports £40,000 [9]. This money was put to good effect by Bill, who used it to fund the UK Type approval of the AX3, and, after around two years attained CAA section S approval to manufacture the aircraft in the UK during 1992. Bill dealt directly with the CAA to attain this approval and performed the flight test programme himself. This was of course conditional on Bill completing a short flight test course, which Bill recalls was not exactly a lengthy endeavour:

"The CAA even allowed me to carry out the flight test programme after I took a short test flight course with Air Vice Marshall Merriman, and I mean short!"

The world of aviation was intrigued by the new aircraft, and in particular, the microlight community. The November/December 1992 issue reported:

"After something like two years- and it must have seemed far longer- Bill Sherlock of Cyclone Airsports has finally got the French-designed AX3 side-by-side two-seater through Section S. He thus joins Mainair in the elite club of manufacturers who produce both fixed-wing and flexwing aircraft.

Bill has kept a typically low profile while the work has been proceeding, mainly because he preferred to proceed in easy and affordable stages.

The finished aircraft is very similar to the machine demonstrated at Popham in March 1991, except that the four-stroke has been replaced by a Rotax 582. It will return eventually, as an option. The price, however, has increased markedly and at £14,808 including VAT is nowhere near the £9000 Bill originally aimed at.

Although regarded as a French design nowadays, the AX3 is actually a heavily developed version of the Weedhopper designed by American John Chotia in the very early days of microlighting. The American model was significant in that it was the first microlight to boast a purpose-designed engine, rather than the chainsaw/snowmobile/you-name -it units pressed into service by other manufacturers. The Chotia engine, however, was a dreadful power plant which did the aircraft no favours at all, and it was not until the design rights crossed the Atlantic that the aircraft's true potential could be realised." [10]

The details in this article are puzzling as both Bill Sherlock and Graeme Park dispute the installation of a Rotax 582 in the AX3 at that time.

Bill recalls: *"We never fitted a four-stroke engine to the AX3, apart from experimental Rotax 508, and we never fitted a Rotax 582. We did however, fit the Rotax 532 70 BHP and the Powervalve Rotax 618 to a couple of aircraft. The Rotax 582 engine came with the advent of the AX2000, which also later had the option of the four-stroke HKS engine."*

Graeme Park: *"The reference to the Rotax 582 is strange since my (G-MYHG), and most of the early AX3s in the UK, were powered by the Rotax 503. And that is still the case if you look at G-INFO! I thought the first AX3 that I came across with a 582 was G-MYER (that Hugh Know flew from Shetland to Norway etc.) but note that it is now classed as an AX2000. There is also at least one AX2000 still registered with a HKS but sure that it was the four stroke 508 in the AX3 because the same issue of Microlight Flying lists the other Cyclone Airsports product of the time, the Chaser, with a 508 option (instead of the 377 or 447)."*

In fact, G-MYER was not to be fitted with a Rotax 582 until later in her life and did the trip to Norway with a Rotax 503 as her powerplant. The 582 and the AX3 were only ever paired as a proof of concept for the later AX2000.

Bill continues: *"G-MYER had a 503 when it flew to Norway. It was only ever fitted with a 582 under test conditions as a proof of concept for the AX2000. The AX2000 was a different airframe from the AX3 and G-MYER was used to try various pre-production modifications for the AX2000, before finally becoming redesignated as an AX2000."*

As for the Rotax 508, this was only mated to the AX3 for a short experimental period of about a week. It was just not powerful enough to provide the grunt necessary to carry two people. Once the AX2000 came along, the four-stroke HKS600E engine was fitted to several aircraft including one at York Microlight Centre. This aircraft actually had its engine overhauled at 2000 hours by Bill himself at Cyclone Airsports.

In early 1993, Cyclone Airsports Ltd purchased Pegasus Aviation/Solar Wings, and moved from Drayton St. Leonard to

Manton, Marlborough. Until now, the AX3 had been manufactured from a kit supplied by Marc Mathot at Ultralair, France. Sadly, they went into receivership in 1993, and so manufacture of the parts was transferred to Manton. The company was by now called Cyclone Airsports Ltd – Trading as Pegasus Aviation. It was at Manton in later years that the AX2000 was developed.

Paul Dewhurst completed the first flight test of the new AX3 for the BMAA in the May/June 1994 edition of Microlight Flying magazine. A very positive review by Paul reported that the aircraft had good performance and manners, although he wasn't keen on the "Walt Disney Styling" [11]. During this year the aircraft also had its first North Sea crossing as part of that two-ship formation flown in aid of Amnesty International by Tom Grieve and Hugh Knox. This flight also won the BMAA's Steve Hunt Trophy for the most outstanding flight of 1994.

During 1995, also in G-MYER, Bill was involved in flying a challenge for a popular Saturday evening TV show, You Bet! The show had been around in various guises since the late 80s. Originally it had been fronted by Bruce Forsyth, but in the 90s the presenting duties fell to Matthew Kelly.

The premise was that Bill had to fly over and under a course of hurdles set at five metre heights while his colleague, David, in the passenger seat tried to throw balls into nets set on the ground.

This, I'm sure, was not an easy thing to do when travelling at 50mph and going up and down over and under hurdles in a microlight, as you do!

After Matthew had introduced the challenge, as was the normal format for this show, the panel guests were asked to 'place their bets' on whether Bill and David could succeed. Three went for 'No', with only one having confidence in Bill and his fragile looking machine. The studio audience were more confident though with a resounding 62% voting 'Yes'.

Switching from the studio to the recorded challenge and the result was never in doubt. Bill flew the AX3 superbly, and his colleague, missed only one shot, netting the 10 they needed in five passes of the course with an extra one for good luck [12].

The film looked quite spectacular and was exactly the sort of challenge popular with early evening Saturday TV at the time. Things were looking promising for Bill's machine, and a TV appearance cannot have harmed his chances of ensuring that the AX3 became the Cessna 152 of the microlight world.

That was the show from the TV audience perspective. What they did not know was...... and this is where Bill takes up the story again:

"During practice the previous week, it had been quite windy, and the groundspeeds over the course had been much slower than for the later televised event. I'd developed a technique where I'd close the throttle towards the top of the climb over the goal post and as the power decayed put the nose down to fly under the next goal post while adding full throttle. On one occasion during practice I'd miss-timed adding the throttle, and stalled into the ground under the goal post causing damage. David and the crew at Cyclone Airsports had one week to put the aircraft back together for the actual show.

It had been David who'd got us into this stunt, because a few weeks before he had himself led a challenge with his racing hovercraft. So, the fact that he had to work pretty much all night for that week putting the aircraft back together was his fault."

I hadn't appreciated what a colourful and interesting history I would discover during my research into the history of the AX3 for this book. For those interested, the clip from You Bet! can be found on YouTube and I've included the link in the references section.

The Flylight Years

Recalling my mention of Paul Dewhurst's flight test in the previous chapter, leads me nicely into where Yankee Lima started her life back in the mid-90s. Yankee Lima is what you would call a 'well-loved aeroplane'. In fact, a chance conversation with Chris Copple the CFI at Mainair, who was the examiner for my initial GST back in 2014, revealed he had actually flown Yankee Lima as well. In fact, he had flown his Flight Instructor test in her in the mid-90s! Small world!

Yankee Lima now has over 3600 hours on her airframe and has had several engines bolted to the front to pull her into the sky. In fact, I imagine if you checked the provenance of all of the component parts within her structure, she would be very similar to Trigger's broom in Only Fools and Horses!

As an aside, I recently discovered when reading Dave Bremner's excellent book, 'Bristol Scout 1264: Rebuilding Granddad's Aircraft' that in order for an aircraft to qualify as an original aircraft it only needs one or two original parts on it, provided you can prove that those parts were definitely part of the original aeroplane. In his case, he built his replica Bristol Scout from the control column, rudder bar and magneto from his granddad's aircraft – which we presume his granddad had kept as mementoes of his time in the RFC during the First World War. Sadly, as he couldn't prove the connection of those parts to the original aircraft, it has to be classed as a replica, but if he had the documentation, it would be considered a rebuild of the original aircraft! [13]

Every day's a school day!

Yankee Lima was initially a flying school aircraft and did the majority of those 3600 hours training new pilots and instructors at Flylight in Sywell.

Ben Ashman is one of the instructors at Flylight and he, like many others who have flown her, has a story or two about Yankee Lima; an aeroplane he describes as:

"like a lovely, compassionate aunt. Always looking after whoever flew with her."

One of his most memorable incidents occurred after a student he was instructing had got disorientated whilst flying Yankee Lima solo. This had led to the student electing to make a precautionary landing in a full field of rape, presenting quite a logistical problem for the retrieval of Yankee Lima, which at the time was fully utilised at Flylight as a training aircraft and as such could not be left on the ground for any length of time.

The choices were simple.

Either they would have to drive out to the field and derig her, removing the wings and possibly tail plane in order to trailer her back to their home airfield at Sywell, which would then require some time to be spent re-rigging. Alternatively, they could retrieve her from the aforementioned field full of rape by flying her out.

No contest really – the decision was simple – they were going to fly her out and Ben was the man who was quickly "volun-told" for the dubious honour of this task due to the unfortunate fact that he was the lightest instructor at Flylight at that time.

On arriving at the field Ben surveyed the area trying to find the best spot for an improvised runway. With a sigh of relief, he located a small patch of earth where the rape hadn't grown. At least now they had a runway, of sorts...

This "runway" was approximately 40 metres long which if you are familiar with the POH of the AX3 is 20 metres short of the "book" take-off roll of 60 metres and 50 metres short of the distance required to clear a 15-metre object, not that rape is a plant that grows to 15 metres tall; in fact the only plant I can think of that grows that high is a Trifid, and there were none of those around in Popham at that time.

Either way it was going to be tight.

Very tight.

Having carefully ensured the aircraft was down to minimum weight and keeping the fuel to the bare minimum, Ben turned into wind and lined up. Fingers firmly crossed, he applied full power and accelerated towards the rape. As the rape started to fill the windscreen and the sky was almost nowhere to be seen Yankee Lima got airborne, skimming the tops of the rape plants as she climbed into the sky.

Ben recalls: *"It was close, but we got off OK, with rape plants dangling from the undercarriage."*

Another of the tales that Yankee Lima would tell, if she could speak, is one that is probably common to quite a few AX3 owners.

When I first sat inside the cockpit, I noticed that there was a permanent pervading smell of petrol. I guess this is not really very surprising as the fuel tanks are strapped to the seats directly behind you, but in the case of Yankee Lima, there may be a more specific reason for the smell that my children delightfully refer to as "aeroplane smell". I got chatting with former Yankee Lima pilot and ex-RAF Commanding Officer at RAF Wittering, Paul Higgins – he has some pleasant memories flying YL:

"I did 6 happy lessons in her as a student back in 2003; great fun and fond memories!"

As an ex-senior RAF officer Paul has flown in many fast jets including the Hawk, Harrier, Jaguar and Tornado, with quite a few sorties in Harriers in particular:

"I first flew Yankee Lima back in June 2003 with Dave Broom, (I was one of his first students)" and comparing his time flying in fast jets with Yankee Lima "none match up to the sheer delight [and] connectivity with the task of flying and simplicity associated with Yankee Lima - great fun."

But returning to that popular microlight pilot fragrance - eau de petrol:

"My most memorable trip was with Ben Ashman who I flew with to sort out an odd post-first solo inconsistency with my landings - I overfilled Yankee Lima with petrol and it managed to cover Ben when we were flying - I think it took all of Ben's professionalism to stop him from murdering me in the air! Got

there in the end [with the landings] and I remember happy times getting to know Yankee Lima."

Ben can't remember much about it (it was 15 years ago), but can attest to the fact that petrol and skin are not a good mix, recalling: *"when you leant back and if the tank was over filled, the fuel will leak out of the breather tube and down the instructors back. Stings like hell!"*

Graham Richardson is another former student who also learnt to fly at Sywell in Yankee Lima in the early 2000s. He recalls stories that I'm sure sound familiar to many pilots, like the first time he took YL through an inversion layer. For non-pilots, an inversion layer is where the air below is colder than the air above (air normally cools as it gets higher and further away from the Earth). In an inversion this means that the air below can't rise and therefore gets murky with pollution, cigarette smoke, car exhausts etc. all trapped. This causes a haze that is difficult to see through.

Graham takes up the story:

"As we approached the inversion layer you could see it was a layer, but only a thin crown layer at the top of the murk below. As we climbed through it, it suddenly became gin clear, with blue sky and the sun shining. Here and there were small humps where the air, becoming a little warmer was trying to break through the layer, but couldn't."

"Everywhere one looked was like I imagined the North or South Pole to be – one vast, flat expanse of white, broken only by the humps of clouds trying to break through. I said to Colin, my instructor, don't ask me to do anything for at least ten minutes 'cos I'm just admiring the desolate splendour of it all!"

"Then when descending, I was overwhelmed with a sense of dread as we approached the layer again. From above it looked solid enough to land on so I tensed myself for the bump of a heavy landing, which of course never came!

Fabulous! It's a shame you only get to experience that once."

Still appealing to the internet to help me in my search for tall tales and nostalgia involving Yankee Lima, Dave Wallington answered my call.

"In September '98 I was on a check flight with Ben of Flylight, out of Sywell. I had yet to take my GST, so I was still mopping up information and experience. It was quite a breezy morning, so having climbed to the overhead Ben took the controls, with an air of 'watch this, Dave'.

Into wind, he applied plenty of power and raised the nose sufficiently to put us on the point of stalling. At this stage the airfield wasn't going by at any speed - in fact it started going the 'wrong' way! We were flying backwards. In groundspeed, anyway. Mustering as much composure as I could, I asked Ben if we should be looking out of the front or the back. We were smiling for the rest of the trip.

Dave Wallington with Yankee Lima

And we've all had those 'fuel' moments, especially in an aircraft whose forward momentum can be severely diminished if there is more than even a breath of wind. In Dave's case it ended up with several unscheduled landings to refuel, as at the time Yankee Lima was still a single tank, 28 litre aircraft which provided for limited range.

Some four years later, after Paul sold the Flylight Shadow, my flying buddy and I opted to 'do' Popham for the May weekend jamboree. This time in 'YL'. Paul advised us to stash some spare fuel around the airframe, as we were unlikely to be able to complete the trip on her single tank. The journey down saw us at Oakley, topping up from our can, arriving at a busy Popham with 1 hour 40 in the log. Easy, or so we thought...

Saturday evening saw off any hope of my buddy being sober enough to fly YL back to Sywell the next day. And Sunday was forecast to be a stiff headwind, so we were advised to head back earlier, rather than later. After topping up the can (twice) at the local gas station, we tried our luck with mother nature. Progress was painfully slow, and after fifty minutes or so, dropped into Chiltern Park, just south of Benson. In a strengthening wind, our optimism about hitting Sywell next plummeted, as we laboured past Buckingham, the 503 singing away, whilst gulping our dwindling get home options. Our remaining choice was to call in at Finmere, the site of my first solo cross-country, some years before. Our landing roll was commendably short. In fact well short, as there was a Sunday market in the next field! Another hour and 5 minutes.

After dumping the last few litres of two-stroke mix into YL, we were airborne again, hardly noticed by the bargain-seekers nearby. Approaching Sywell we requested, and received, a straight in approach and landed. While we were putting YL away in an almost deserted hangar (everyone else was still at Popham!) we observed that the next pilot of G-MYYL would need to add "some" fuel before flight. Total time from Popham was two hours 50 minutes!

Apart from the obvious lessons learned, we did develop our ability to consider options available en route - particularly judging field type and size for an unplanned landing. Something we have never forgotten..."

The final word in this chapter from the many who have flown her at Flylight goes to Ben Ashman, though:

"Yankee Lima is a true lady, never outrageous, always well-mannered and had a host of admirers.

All at Flylight loved her, me included."

Into Private Ownership

After a lifetime of being used and abused by student pilots learning the basics of flight, YL had now earned her retirement from teaching – or so she thought. So, after a student misjudged their landing once more, causing the fragile nosewheel to collapse and damaging the front of the plane, and with a heavy heart, the owners at Flylight decided to sell her on to her first private owners, father and son duo, Douglas and Adam Bedborough. Both Adam and Douglas knew her well anyway as they were already flying Yankee Lima: Douglas as a qualified NPPL and Adam not far behind in his learning. She would still be a familiar face, though, as they were based at Sywell, so at least it wasn't too much of a move.

It was spring 2005, and Adam and Douglas had plans for some exciting flying to be done, but first there was the little matter of Adam completing his training! Poor old Yankee Lima. There she was, all ready for a nice relaxing retirement, with some nice sleepy visits to local farm strips for a cup of tea and a Hobnob. And yet, with a bang, it was back to reality and back to work.

It was around this time that they decided Yankee Lima's range needed extending. After a bit of research and with some help from Paul Dewhurst they fitted a dual fuel tank modification. This would increase the fuel capacity from 28 litres to 48 litres, and consequently flight endurance could now be as much as three hours with reserve (if your bum can put up with the 'seats' for that length of time).

Adam and friend, Oli en-route to Sywell from Shobdon in 2006. Note the bungees over their heads that hold the doors closed!

During 2006, Adam and his friend Oli took YL to the annual microlight fly in at Sywell. In the photo opposite, they are enjoying themselves so much that they both forgot to look at the map and quickly got lost, somewhere over wales. Ah, the happy pre-GPS days…

Adam and Douglas both passed their General Skills Tests in Yankee Lima and owned and flew her for around three years, finally selling her on in mid-2008.

It was at this point, that she was sold on to Clive Fletcher. Clive lived in Norfolk and during this time Yankee Lima was moved to a local airstrip, Priory Farm. Clive was the owner until late 2011.

Her next owner was a Scotsman, Roy Ferguson. However, sadly she spent much of the next seven years of her life in the hangar, earning the unenviable reputation as 'the hangar queen'. Tom Garnham, who purchased her from Roy, recalls: *"Every year he would come down and work on Yankee Lima to get her ready for her permit inspection. And every year after he had done this, she would fail the permit, and so she stayed in the hangar."*

Eventually, clearly Roy had had enough and decided to sell on the AX3, and Tom was there to purchase her. Tom, an HGV driver by trade, had wanted to get back into flying since he'd seen a Shadow land in his field. It rekindled his interest in flying since he had let his PPL lapse 23 years earlier. After making a few enquiries about which hoops he would have to jump through, he discovered how the red tape that normally bars entry to these things was surprisingly scant. So, just a GST and self-declaration medical and he was good to go.

When he saw the advert for YL, he jumped at the chance to purchase her as she also came with that other most valuable commodity in the South East: a hangar space! During early 2017, Tom carried out numerous jobs on YL to get her back to flying standard, and then had the dreaded inspection, including the wince-inducing 'Betts' test – if you've ever witnessed this you'll know what I mean. Happily, she passed the skin test but did fail on a number of minor items, including a lack of 'no smoking' signing… However, by mid-April, all jobs had been completed and now Tom was free to take his new plane to the skies.

Tom Garnham and father (also Tom!) enjoying Yankee Lima a few months before I bought her

Happiness is owning your own aircraft!

Since then Tom has gone on to purchase and fly the aircraft that got him back into the skies, owning and flying a Streak Shadow, and has now returned to Group A flying a Rollason Condor.

A Frustrating Year on the Ground

The weather.

The bloody great British weather.

From the end of September 2017 until around March 2018 the North West of England experienced its own version of the monsoon season. It rained, rained, rained and the wind howled and blew such that we thought it would never end. This was something 'special' even for us Lancastrians, who are accustomed to perpetually unsettled weather. On the occasions when the wind didn't blow, the runway at Rossall was almost always unusable due to the amount of rain that had fallen. On the even more rare occasions when the runways had drained, it wasn't raining and the wind was suitable, then either I was unavailable, or James was unavailable.

I've already mentioned that I didn't legally need an instructor to go up with me, but felt it would be foolish to take those first few flights without one, in an unfamiliar aeroplane, with significantly different flying characteristics to those I had flown before.

In fact, when I did get to fly with James, there were several elements to his briefing that I would not have considered, such as the propeller rotating in the opposite direction to a Rotax 912, and therefore a bootful of right rudder is not going to help straighten up on the take-off roll. Or that the high thrust line induces a slight pitch down moment when you increase the throttle to go around, so you need to be mindful of positive back pressure on the stick, or else come face to face with mother earth sooner than you intended.

September turned to October and before I knew it, it was January. But I continued to wait it out, contenting myself with renting school aircraft (from Barton) and spending time doing small jobs to YL over the winter months.

One thing that had been bugging me was that the panel didn't have any coloured markings on the gauges to help sight read your air speed so I purchased a set from Skydrive and set about cleaning up the gauges, removing all the tatty old bits of tape and replacing with new red, yellow and green instrument gauge markings. I'd also noted that the cockpit placards, well, bits of paper sellotaped to the panel were looking, well, like bits of paper taped to the panel.

A bit of googling and help from fellow aviators pointed me to a website that will custom make laser cut plastic signs to your spec for very reasonable prices, so I had a set made and this further improved the look of the cockpit.

In my final act of cockpit pimpage (that just sounds wrong doesn't it?) I ordered some red anodised alloy instrument screws to replace the rusty steel ones.

The result speaks for itself: much tidier.

New anodised screws, instrument markings, custom laser cut signs and a tablet for SkyDemon - YL moves into the 21st Century

A few engine jobs were completed, replacing some rubbers on the airbox and fuel pump, and I also added the pièce de résistance: some custom made 'Harriet' decals to the outside of the pod on either side.

I also ran the engine relatively frequently, as in my experience internal combustion engines are not happy if they don't get used regularly.

Still, by mid-March, the stars had not aligned, and now the permit was about to expire.

No bother, I'd done a ton of work on her over the winter and she'd been hangered and covered the whole time.

How could she possibly fail?

She failed.

Permit me to fly?

It had all been going so well.

I'd spent an inordinate amount of time, blood, sweat, tears, oh yes, and money, on Harriet since I bought her late that previous summer.

In fact, if you calculated the purchase price, hangarage, transport costs, and other spend to date I think my first flying hour was looking like costing me around £4500! The next one should only be £2250, though, and I hear it gets progressively closer to the average helicopter hourly rate shortly after that, or so I hope….

Double or triple A rated, these aircraft investment funds are! So, if you want to make a small fortune*, check them out at an airfield/investment bank near you!

* Investors should note that in order to qualify for this once-in-a lifetime opportunity, you will need a large fortune to start with. Also, I am not regulated or authorised by the Financial Conduct Authority or able to give financial advice.

So, the night before 'the big day', James had sent me the image below of Yankee Lima rolled out in all her glory ready to be poked and prodded and pulled at by the inspector.

Harriet – nervously waiting for her annual check up

I wasn't too worried, as I hadn't flown her since her last inspection and she was checked over by a BMAA inspector before I bought her last year. I guess the only thing on my mind was the dreaded Betts test, as the skins on her are original and nothing lasts forever.

Around noon on Permit Day, James called to let me know everything was going ok, and also to check that I had the fuel pump and air box rubber mounts ready to fit, which I did, and fitted soon afterwards.

I hung up and went back to work, although in reality this involved pacing up and down the office floor like an expectant father, day-dreaming about all the adventures I was going have this weekend with Harriet.

Unable to contain myself and on my fifth coffee I glared accusingly at the phone.

"Ring! Why won't you bloody ring?"

Eventually my iPhone announced that James was on the phone by bouncing along my desk emitting a noise like a trapped angry wasp.

It was not the news I was hoping for:

"A couple of small issues."

My heart sank as I continued reading the text:

"Unfortunately, this bracket will need to be replaced…"

At this point I stopped reading and looked at the accompanying picture.

The troublesome hole in the trailing edge bracket has elongated

And just like that, my dreams of soaring through the skies with Harriet during the next few weeks evaporated into a solid mist of disappointment.

I also realised that this would also mean further, erm, "investment" in my now triple A rated (honest) subprime aircraft-based mortgage bond. An investment so solid it is guaranteed to pay out no profit whatsoever, fact!

Merrill Lynch, JP Morgan and Goldman Sachs, your brokers ain't got nothing on this one!

So, the trailing edge bracket needed replacing. Everything else was fine, including the Betts test! No other problems, but unfortunately the hole in the bracket which the pin goes through to secure the trailing edge to the fuselage had elongated (not sure how that was missed on the previous inspection, given that she had not flown since, but anyway...). Therefore, the bracket needed replacing, and crying about it wasn't going to change that.

And if I'm honest, I guess I was grateful that we had found the issue sooner rather than an alternative scenario where the wing could have unilaterally decided to implement its own form of Brexit from the remainder of the airframe. In this version I'd get a cameo appearance playing the envious role of the European Union's chief negotiator desperately trying to hold everything together in the cockpit as the altimeter counted down to my own personal 'transition' period.

I'm not gonna lie, that wasn't really on my bucket list.

So now all I needed to do was to get her fixed...

James helpfully located the supplier of the parts, which turned out to be a reasonable price, so as a precaution I replaced both sides, even though only one had failed. This was an attempt to stave off any potential for a future referendum by Yankee Lima's wings on, err, 'WEXIT'... Actually, that doesn't really work does it? I'll leave the EU metaphors alone from now on, I promise.

The only thing I needed at this point were the parts! It'd been three weeks since Yankee Lima was grounded, and as "luck" would have it, I was home quite a bit, but unfortunately the parts supplier took a bit of time to ship them and consequently no flight was still occurring!

Still, I was getting closer to the end of this particular obstacle course now, and the summer had to be just around the corner...right?

Flight at Last!

At this point, we re-join the story where we began, sitting on the runway on a very breezy day with the engine running and James and I looking at each other.

James made the call.

"F*** it, let's go for it."

I pushed the oversized throttle lever fully forwards and as Yankee Lima started to accelerate, I felt her start to come to life. The acceleration wasn't exactly punishing, but I suppose there were two fully grown men and plenty of fuel on board fighting with the Rotax's 50 horses and Newton's third law of physics.

James had briefed me to keep the nose low as soon as we got airborne, to let the speed build, so as soon as I felt us lift off, I checked the control column slightly and glanced down at the ASI to confirm that it was rotating clockwise.

Best climb speed is around 50mph, and as soon as we reached that speed, I raised the nose and climbed straight ahead while I started to get acquainted with the different flight characteristics, compared to anything else I had flown. Turning crosswind, James and I conferred and quickly came to the conclusion that it was too windy to continue the flight and the decision was taken to end the flight after one circuit, assuming I got the approach and landing correct.

Turning onto final I flew a long, powered approach towards 02 and with a bit of assistance from James, landed on the numbers. Taxying back and shutting down was a surreal feeling. It had only been a single dual circuit, but I was thrilled after nearly a year of owning her to finally be able to take Harriet flying.

I then posed in the cockpit for the obligatory photo call of a happy owner/pilot.

She flies!!!

One thing I do recall (and this is a bit of a theme that is repeated later) is that I needed to work on my rudder/aileron coordination more. The AX3 is less forgiving than more modern microlights if you are not fleet of foot!

I didn't care though; I had flown my aeroplane!

Time to Go Solo

Over the years, I am certain that hundreds of students have flown their first solo in Yankee Lima, after all she was at Sywell for many years training students.

An article I had written for Microlight Flying magazine (the best flying magazine in the country, I am reliably informed by the unbiased objective editor, Geoff Hill) had gained a bit of attention from another former pilot, Graham Richardson. He'd written to me to say he was delighted to see Yankee Lima was still flying and that he'd had many fun experiences and adventures in her.

I asked him to share his first solo story, although technically it was his second solo as the first was at Desborough Airfield (an ex-Second World War bomber station near Corby where the microlights used the perimeter track as a runway), in a Hiway Skytrike back in the late 1970s. Back then, you didn't even need a microlight licence to fly, as there was no such thing! You simply flew, assisted by instructors who "knew a bit more than you, and were still alive." Despite this experience, Graham was not put off and in the early Noughties (this is apparently how the first few years of the new millennium are referred to these days) headed to Sywell in search of gaining the newly CAA issued microlight license with Flylight.

Finally, there were "reliable" two-seat microlights that you could train on; the only decision left to make was whether to go weight-shift or three-axis.

Ten seconds sitting in Yankee Lima made Graham's decision an easy one. Three-axis, thank you!

Graham began his training with Ben Ashman, and as he already had some experience from his hair-raising flights in the 70s, they began the microlight syllabus on lesson three.

I thought about writing this from Graham's own notes, but it sounds so much better in his own voice, so I've reproduced it pretty much as he wrote it. Graham's story encapsulates what a first solo feels like and describes the emotions beautifully:

"So, I turn up at Sywell for my lesson and ask Colin, my instructor, if we can do more PFLs today. 'No,' he says, 'circuits today'. I'm simultaneously disappointed (no PFLs) and apprehensively excited – maybe solo if my flying proves to be not too bad. I check out 'YL as usual, but this time I check the float bowls – no problem there except I dislodge the air filter getting at them. Oh dear, Colin has to rescue me and acquires black hands just like mine!

Eventually it's all done (Colin ribs me a bit – 'must be a record, 45 minutes for a pre-flight inspection') and we set off. My first circuit is crap but I'm soon up to speed.

'When you do go solo,' says Colin, 'that's a good field from here if you get an engine failure.' Hint one, 'from here, I'd go into that one' and so on, all round the circuit (hint numbers two and three etc.).

We do a glide approach, a powered approach, a short field landing 'as soon as possible after the markers' (hint number six,) we touch down just after the markers, Colin says 'go,' and we accelerate away as usual. Colin's hand hovers over the PTT on climb out (hint number seven) but he says nothing – someone else is on the radio. They finish – power's gone, Colin to tower: 'Golf Yankee Lima practice fan stop.' I push the nose down, we have airspeed and runway ahead, and Colin is satisfied with my power failure on take-off (hint number eight).

Finally, we land full stop. Even now, with all these hints (eight) I didn't cotton on and taxied back to Flylight, but Colin says 'don't go past the tower and all that mucky bit, park outside the windows this side' (hint nine). I check the mags and switch off.

I'm about to undo the harness when Colin says, 'hold on, I'm getting out..., not you.' He probably didn't say it exactly like that but you get the gist of it – gulp, this is it. He's sending me solo.

Oh my God!

He says all the things you know he'll say about taxying being easier, better acceleration, greater climb rate, control sensitivity etc, and I try to listen.

Then he's gone.

'Don't forget the doors,' he shouts.

I dutifully twang the bungees together.

He's gone.

It's quiet.

Right, start-up checks. – STAMP – Security, Throttle, All clear to start, Mags on, clear Prop. Even as I shout 'Clear Prop', I still cover the mic so as not to deafen… who?

No-one else here.

This feels weird, it's not me here, surely?

Engine starts OK, I call the tower 'Sywell Information, this is Microlight Golf Mike Yankee Yankee Lima request radio check and taxi for circuit.' Did I say circuit or circuits? Colin said to do only one circuit unless the approach was crap or the runway obstructed etc.

With clearance from the tower it's time to go, and I'm off on something scarier than Blackpool's Big One.

I taxi sedately, anxious not to foul up at this stage. Near the hold, I turn into wind and do the pre-take-off checks, that I won't bore you with here, except to say that it didn't seem to take as long as when Colin's aboard!

I taxi to the holding point and call the tower: 'Golf Yankee Lima ready for departure.'

My God, who are you kidding?

'Golf Yankee Lima, take-off at your discretion, surface wind is…' – I don't remember now, and I probably only half heard then (only joking). We're (sorry I'm) on the centreline of 25 (Actually just to the right of it, where I should be – 'don't go over the white bits' Colin always says).

Smoothly, I open the throttle, full revs on the counter and we're (I'm) off...

We (look I can't get the hang of I, rather than we, so I'll use we but now it simply means me and Yankee Lima) lift off and rocket up at what seems like a phenomenal rate for Yankee Lima. Just goes to show what a difference unnecessary baggage makes (sorry, sorry, I didn't mean it Colin, but couldn't resist)!

As I turn crosswind, we're already up to 1000', so I level off, and head for the next reference point. Check airspeed, check height, it's a lot livelier on the controls and I tend to be a bit heavy handed.

Downwind, I call the tower and the reply is 'Golf Yankee Lima one in front, report final.' I spend what seems like forever looking, but eventually, spot a weight shift turning final.

Fuel ok.

Harness ok.

Height ok.

Airspeed ok.

Check next reference point, avoid overflying village, listen to radio (shame it's not The Archers, an everyday tale of, oh where was I?). This circuit is turning out to be a bit higher than previous ones; don't turn base leg too early.

On base leg I descend at 60 indicated, height looks ok, perhaps a bit too high and I begin to turn final and prepare to inform the tower. At that moment someone on the ground calls the tower to ask for clearance to taxi.

Ok, I'll wait until he's finished and try again. As I'm about to call, the tower calls me 'Golf Yankee Lima land at your discretion, surface wind is...'

I'm surprised that I'm a little peeved at being pipped at the post as it were, but at the same time I was pleased and proud that the tower made no fuss about what they might have thought was a forgotten radio call, knowing that I was a student on his first solo.

I am even more pleased to get an unexpected 'Golf Yankee Lima congratulations' after a pretty good landing under the circumstances. A heartfelt 'Golf Yankee Lima, thank you very much,' is all I can say as I taxy back in sheer disbelief at the anticlimatic feel of it all.

Did I really do that?

Back at the Flylight hangar I stop, check the mags and switch off, unbuckle and climb out (perhaps clamber would be more appropriate as I'd never managed it in anything other than an ungainly fashion!).

I turn good old Yankee Lima into wind and stroll nonchalantly back to Colin who is waiting outside to explain why I didn't call 'Final'.

'Well done mate.'

'Cheers, mate.'

Handshakes – pause. 'I did it!'

I hug Colin, hoping no one is looking, we're both smiling.

What a day!

Graham Richardson in the cockpit of YL, note the three-bladed propeller

Rossall Field 25th June 2018, just four years and 13 days after my original first solo at Barton was an amazing day.

The day I flew my first solo in my own aircraft!

I awoke early and quickly checked the weather at Rossall: 'High gust 4mph.'

It was on. I was going flying.

As I drove North, I wondered if today would be the day I got to fly my aircraft solo. Upon arrival, James' briefing was, erm, brief:

"To be honest, one good landing and I'm getting out, mate, after the way you flew in the challenging conditions the other week."

Motivation indeed.

So, with nil wind we elected to use 02 as it has more options in the event of an engine failure. Take-off and the circuit went well, all the while James was pointing out possibilities in the event of an engine failure, which to be honest in Yankee Lima at 700 feet consist of a quick glance at the field beneath your feet…

And then after lining up and doing a little sideslip (I was a bit rusty) I performed a good landing (well great if you go by the pilot's official definition, as not only was I alive but you could reuse the plane) and James turned to me.

"Well done. Do you want to backtrack and do another then?" I thought for a few seconds, and feeling quite happy with how I had flown I bit the bullet.

"I think I'm happy to go on my own."

So, with that settled, James jumped out and I taxied to the threshold ready for my first solo circuit in Yankee Lima, my own plane. I still couldn't quite believe it.

Full power applied and a little left rudder to keep her straight on the runway (remember, the prop turns the other way to the Rotax 912), I found as expected that she accelerated much better with only one person on board. The 50 horses in the Rotax 503 were pulling nicely and she lifted off beautifully in very little distance before settling into the climb nicely.

That first circuit was OK, but I did perform a go-around instead of touching down as I was way too high. On my second I did accomplish something that could be loosely described as a landing, or more accurately an 'arrival', but this ended with a slight excursion off the runway to the left. YL required far more positive control inputs than I had been used to up until this point, especially at lower speeds. Still, with only my pride wounded, and crucially, no clubhouse witnesses enthusiastically brandishing scorecards, I backtracked and went again.

My third landing was tolerable, but I went around again on my fourth circuit as I over controlled and ended up ballooning. However, my fifth and final circuit ended with a lovely steady approach and a well held off landing. And so, with time running out before I had to go back to real life and cease being simply a pilot – but also a boyfriend and father – I called it a day and parked YL back up in the hangar with a fatherly smile.

That first solo circuit session in Yankee Lima taught me a few things that are more apparent in an older, flapless, low power high drag aeroplane:

1. If you're too high you can't just dump the flaps out and dive like a Stuka for the threshold, you need to pay more attention to your approach and use side-slipping technique if you are too high. I was out of practice with side-slipping…

2. It's a two-stroke, so temperatures are even more important to watch than they were before, on more modern aircraft – and they are very important there too!

3. Glide approaches are harder to judge, certainly for me they were, as again, there are no flaps to get you out of jail if you are too high once you are 'in'.

4. Trimming works in the opposite sense to how you would expect, so its push forwards for nose up and pull back for nose down, not one to get wrong when you are close to the ground.

5. Rudder - there is one, and you need to use it, or you will quickly know about it. In a Eurostar or a C42 of course you use the rudder, but it's more of a nod towards it than actually using your feet. In the AX3, if you don't use the rudder the aircraft simply wallows around pointing its nose in the opposite direction to which you are trying to turn.

Driving back to Rochdale was bliss. Not only had I flown solo in my own aeroplane but I had also learnt a lot from my five circuits, both about YL and also about some areas in my own flying skills that needed some attention. Flying modern microlights does let you get away with a lot more than my old 390kg microlight.

Adventures and Misadventures

Since that first flight and over the last couple of years I've enjoyed quite a few different trips with Harriet, and although her range is not great, we've managed to fly to local farm strips, the beach, an international airport and Manchester's second airport, Barton – the original Manchester Airport before Ringway was built.

Kaz and I flying down the Fylde Coast in Yankee Lima

In fact, thinking back to 2018, even taking passengers has been interesting. On one occasion we'd taxied to the end of runway 02 and, after confirming all was well, I applied full power.

"Oh, it actually flies?" uttered the perpetually unimpressed teenager beside me, as we accelerated through 50mph towards the hedge.

Low expectations or what?

Happily, for Isobel, and indeed for me, fly she did. We soared clear of the hedge at around 100 feet and climbing to go and explore the skies together that day.

All of these trips have been memorable for different reasons.

Whether it's being unable to stop the engine on the beach, landing on the threshold of a mile-long runway and taxying forever to the apron at Blackpool, dodging Typhoons on the way back from Barton or landing at my first fly-in at St Michaels.

I thought it might be fun to share some of those stories here and although some of them have been published before, I hope you will still enjoy them.

Left wing down with a 13-knot crosswind, landing into Kenyon Hall Farm for the 2020 Fly-in – courtesy of Gavin Carr

St Michael's Fly-in

Looking back at my logbook I had less than two hours experience flying YL on the day of the 2018 St Michaels Wings and Wheels fly in. So, it is unsurprising that it turned into one of those days with a lot of firsts.

My first flight away from the safety of the circuit in YL.

My first take-off from runway 28 at Rossall, or as we colloquially call it, the 'short one', it's only 260 metres hedge to hedge.

My first land away in YL.

My first fly-in, in any aircraft.

And, my first group fly-out as well, as I enjoyed the company of several flex wing pilots from Rossall on short the trip to St Michael's.

It was also my first flight to St Michael's, although technically I flew in twice as I had to go around the first time as I rounded out too high whilst still getting used to how low to the ground YL sits. The flights helped to build my experience in my own aeroplane, even if St Michaels is only six nautical miles (NM) to the South East of Rossall Field.

St Michaels 'Wings & Wheels Fly-in 2018

The crosswind landing back at Rossall made me make a mental note that I have to be quick with my feet, that the AX3 likes being flown all the way to the ground and as soon as you round out, that wing acts like a huge airbrake and you very quickly lose flying speed.

It was a lovely day's flying doing exactly what I had bought YL for - namely bimbling about from airfield to airfield and talking rubbish with other pilots over a can of diet coke!

Not the End at Knott End!

It had been three weeks since I had last flown Harriet and I was more than happy when Elektra and I were free to take her up for another adventure. Arriving at Rossall, I noticed several club members were already present and discussing the day's flying, over the inevitable steaming mugs of kick start caffeine. A plan quickly emerged to visit Knott End beach (with the promise of an ice cream for Elektra), which I was excited about as I had never landed on a beach before.

I refuelled Harriet whilst Elektra, dressed in her Red Arrows flying suit, amused herself (and the others) with her cartwheel/handspring/round off flick* repertoire.

* delete as appropriate or feel free to ignore if you are not gymnastically oriented

After the first of our number took-off, I backtracked and departed from runway 02 turning west towards the nearby Pilling Sands microlight site (Knott End beach). Yankee Lima was flying beautifully; she had just had new engine mountings fitted along with her 25-hour service so the engine purred like a happy cat and I noticed on full power, she almost leapt into the air. That could have had something to do with half empty tanks and a passenger who actually weighs about three stone ringing wet... Regardless, this enabled us to climb rapidly to 1500 feet and we continued towards our not too distant destination.

In the vicinity of the upwind end of the beach I glanced down at the unfamiliar moonlike surface and decided not to be the first one down, having not done this before.

"Knott End Traffic, Golf Yankee Lima, orbiting just to the south of Knott End beach. I'm going to watch you guys to see how it's done."

Continuing our orbits, I observed our unofficial flight leader, Andy in his Mainair Blade, skimming low across the beach assessing the surface:

"Looks firm enough to me. Final, number one," he announced confidently and touched down:

"Yep, it's fine Danny."

A couple more aircraft in the group lined up and I descended and joined base leg, calling number three, following the guys in front of me.

On the approach, the feeling of speed was exhilarating as we skimmed low above the sand at about 20ft. The beach looked wet so I continued until I saw tyre tracks. Once I'd locked onto the tracks I flew a little way to check there was no obvious plane-shaped wreckage. Satisfied that the beach was clear of any items that might interest the AAIB and that it looked firm enough I lowered the nose, checking the power slightly and then held off until I felt the main gear caress the sandy surface in a manner that would be totally alien to anyone who has ever flown Ryanair. Why do they always seem so surprised by the runway?

The touchdown was amazing: directly into wind and on a lovely smooth surface. I do, however, continue to forget how little space is needed to land the AX3 and after stopping in less than a football field, I had to taxy for so long that I considered taking off again. Eventually though I arrived at the collection of aluminium and Ultralam machines that denoted the 'Apron'. Happily, this was also adjacent to the ice cream shop.

This is where the fun started.

Before shutting Harriet down, I did my mag drop check to ensure both ignition circuits were working, but nothing happened.

The indicated RPM dropped to 1000 but with no change in the engine note (if you've ever heard/felt a Rotax 503 at 1000rpm, you'd know about it - think minor earthquake – because that's how it feels in the cockpit with a 503 running at 1000 rpm).

Pondering this for a few seconds I concluded I would ask the guys about it, so I'd better shut down.

I turned off both mags and the master switch.

The engine kept turning.

This was a little perplexing to say the least - remember 'pre-ignition' from cars built in the 70s and 80s? Glancing outside, I was aware that everyone was looking at me with expressions that said: "why is he still sitting in his cockpit polluting the atmosphere unnecessarily?"

So, I removed the ignition key and held it up for their inspection through the still stubbornly spinning propeller.

Whilst they pondered that, I thought now what?

TIFS, TIFS, TIFS. The check that we all do when we're about to crash, erm, perform a forced landing in a field. It's an acronym and it goes something like this.

Throttle = Idle.

Ignition = Off.

Fuel!!!

Reaching down to my left I twisted the fuel cock off and waited, comforted by the thought that engines need three things to function: oxygen, ignition and fuel. Remove any of these and the engine will stop, fact.

The engine kept turning.

Sitting there burning my expensive two-stroke fuel/oil mix, I recalled that there is often as much as two minutes of fuel in the fuel lines, so I thought I'd better think of a better solution.

Choke it.

Brilliant! Grinning at my ingenuity I applied full choke, which stopped the engine almost immediately. Phew, was my initial thought, quickly replaced by "I hope it starts again…" as I glanced towards the sea. I also thought it prudent at this point to turn the fuel cock back on again to mitigate against this developing into one of those 'I learnt about flying from that' moments.

Hopping out, I tried to look measured and cool, but was greeted by various quips from the other club members, the best of which was from Joe:

"Alright mate, that took a while, did you drive here?" – as he took delight in referencing my extended taxy.

Following this everyone had a good look at the engine in the way people used to with car engines in the 70s and 80s. You know, push the leads onto the spark plugs, have a look around at nothing in particular to try to determine what's wrong. I half expected someone to suggest we find a pair of tights to replace the fan belt. At least there's no radiator on a 503, so no need to crack an egg into it...

During this exhaustive scientific investigation, I decided to take Red One over to the ice cream shop to get her the promised sweet treat. Walking up the beach I made sure to smile and say a casual hello to some of the other beach users in a manner that suggests this kind of thing is something I do as frequently as breathing.

Sadly though, the ice cream shop was shut, having closed a mere six minutes earlier. My little fast jet pilot was terribly disappointed, but her face brightened when I suggested it simply meant we would have to fly back and land here again one day.

On the beach, smiling, and wondering if she'll start for the return flight...

Upon our return to the beach I discovered two things.

One, no one knew what was up with the mags on my aircraft; and two, a new plan had been concocted to fly across the bay to Bardsea beach. After considering this for a moment, I elected not to participate in my two-stroke single-engine (possibly single-mag) aircraft and decided it would be better to return to Rossall taking in a scenic tour of as many nice, big, flat, empty green airfield-runway-like spaces as possible.

Back in the cockpit, Harriet started first time and I performed my first beach take-off followed by the short flight back to Rossall, which was uneventful.

Later inspection revealed that the problem had been a broken earth, so the mag was always 'On', or is it 'Off'? This bit always confuses me.

Either way, I had been flying on two mags the whole time.

So, another eventful flight for my logbook. My first beach landing and first beach take-off. First tech failure away from my base too. But more importantly, more fantastic memories in an aircraft that was cheaper to buy than a family holiday.

And no criticism from Red One!

A Winter Wonderland

One of the best things about flying and owning your own aircraft is the opportunity to share the experience with others who may never have thought about flying, or not had the chance previously. It was a crisp winter's morning in early 2019 that I was driving over the hills to Rossall Field with my friend Anna. There was snow on the ground, and I had my new 'not-a-Go-Pro' camera in my bag to try out for the first time.

As it was her first flight, and knowing she enjoyed the experience, I asked Anna to contribute to this book, not least of all because I realised that everything I have written so far was lacking in any female input, and I know women definitely like to fly, because I'm married to one!

"On a beautifully crisp day, clear blue sky and sun shining, a day when hope was in abundance, I took my first journey in Harriet. On arriving at the airfield near Lancaster called Rossall Field I was asked to wait in a warm room filled with very knowledgeable, interesting and welcoming pilots and I instantly felt at ease. This was a very big day for me, since being young I'd wanted to fly a plane, not for employment, for the experience. I waited, rather nervously with brew in hand, whilst Danny did all the safety checks. When he was completely satisfied all was in order, I went to meet Harriet.

As I walked up to her, as beautiful as she was, I very nearly turned on my heels. I had butterflies in my tummy and my head was saying (silently, internally), leg it! A day or so earlier, I'd expressed my feelings of maybe not being brave enough to have this experience and a friend simply said, enjoy it. So, with that in my head and complete confidence in Danny and Harriet I just got on with enjoying a superb, exhilarating experience.

Once in the cockpit, Danny explained a number of things to me, including his ability to land in an emergency. Rather than frightening me it simply gave me more confidence in my pilot friend.

Then it was time to position Harriet for take-off. Still on the ground but moving quickly, nose in the air, we took off smoothly. It was a noisy plane, or perhaps it's simply that I'm not used to knowing how noisy or not flying a microlight generally is.

But then the whole experience transformed.

'That' view over Knott End Beach

As Harriet gained altitude, she opened up a whole new world to me. Considering I was 2000 feet in the air and going at 50 miles per hour with what was essentially a fibreglass frame with an engine and wings encasing my body, the beauty of the hills of the Lake District, the sea, the sheer scale of the greenery on the ground, the mapped, grid like, fields, Blackpool Tower in the distance, my breath was taken away.

I've been on big planes before: the first time I journeyed on any plane was from Manchester to Sydney, quite something for a first flight experience. But the flying in Harriet surpassed any other flying experience I've had or am likely to have. There was a calmness. A physical and emotional calmness and a chance to see how beautiful a place we live in, from a whole new perspective. I could see people and things moving around below me – something you only really get on take-off and landing in super-sized passenger planes. Yes, things, people and places appear smaller than they are in 'real life' but you're still aware of how much is going on below you, in every-day life.

Throughout the flight Danny explained a number of technical aspects of the plane itself, as well as flying the plane, of wind speed and its effect on flying speed and so on. All very interesting, again enhancing the experience.

The best part of all was being 2000 feet in the air and just enjoying the panorama. The consciousness of knowing I could do this, be there, without fear and in fact, with a renewed passion for my personal commitment to learn to fly a plane, just for me.

To fulfil a young person's dream, my dream.

One that for a long time seemed unachievable. Now, becoming tangibly attainable."

I love the way that Anna opens her story, although I'm not sure if she was at the same airfield that I fly from, as the airfield she refers to was filled with 'interesting pilots', and not many of us microlight pilots have ever been accused of that when we are talking planes!

And I should also point out that I didn't mention to Anna that I have never actually tested my forced landing capability for real (fingers crossed I never have to), only the usual PFLs we all do from time to time to stay sharp. Still, it was a great flight, the 'not-a-Go-Pro' worked like a dream and I made my first (and so far only) YouTube video set to music to give Anna a permanent reminder of the flight.

A happy Anna with a post flight glow!

Back to Barton

This was my first land away of 2019 in Yankee Lima and my most ambitious trip in her yet. It was quite a windy day, but the southerly wind at 2000' had dropped below 15 knots and that gave me the idea that I might be able to get to Barton and back before going to our evening wedding tasting at the Norton Grange. Kaz does love how efficient I am at managing my schedule like this…

When I arrived at Rossall, there was a fair amount of activity and people milling around so I went about my business pulling YL out and refuelling her to the top.

After a bit of umming and ahing I settled on Barton as the destination instead of Blackpool, which had been my other option. The main factor here for me was that I know Barton well and so I decided to leave Blackpool for another day and made my phone call to Barton for PPR. Of course, the other thing that is tempting about Barton is the refund of the £13.50 landing fee I get as part of my Lancashire Aero Club membership.

The route was simple a straight line from Rossall to Barton with a call to Warton for a MATZ transit and basic service en-route.

Unfortunately, the local weather meant that the overall southerly wind was actually 180 degrees different on the ground at Rossall, so I elected to use 02 for the take-off.

The take-off and climb out went well and I settled into the cruise climb to gradually get me up to around 2500ft by the time I cleared Winter Hill. Checking back on SkyDemon shows that even with the headwind, I managed an average speed of 41 knots over the ground, with a top speed of 53 knots in the descent to Middlebrook Stadium.

Warton were most helpful and it was reassuring to talk with them on my longest flight yet in a two-stroke, where I covered a huge 38 nautical miles en-route to Barton.

Shortly after commencing the descent, I called Barton for joining information and performed a standard overhead join whilst my eyeballs were on stalks looking out for other aircraft as even the Wright Brothers' 1903 Flyer would give YL a run for her money!

An uneventful circuit led me to the approach and I noted the wind was still southerly, whilst trying to perfect my most stable approach in case of any watching eyes from my former instructors in the Mainair offices.

Everything went well right down to the hold off where a gust caused me to balloon slightly, but short blip on the throttle as I had loads of runway left set me up nicely for another go, and this time I set her down just right and taxied off runway 26R for the first time in something other than a school owned C42 or Eurostar!

Yankee Lima at Barton with the historic control tower behind her

Taxying to park behind a Thruster TST (which has no brakes), I leapt out to find Chris and show him my new aeroplane.

A short time later after a quick refreshment in the Veterans Garage café, and paying my landing fee in the tower, and it was time to go. I spotted Marcus as I was doing my pre-take-off checks who gave me a friendly wave and then it was time to depart.

Turning straight onto my North West track I took the time to take a few photographs of familiar land marks from my time learning at Barton, but with my AX3 cockpit in the foreground this time.

Approaching Warton's MATZ they advised me to keep a good look out for a Typhoon that was departing to the East and was climbing through my level. I was all eyes after that call, but I'm not exactly sure what they expected me to be able to do about it if there was a conflict…

Later on, Marcus, who was on frequency, sent me a text:

"AX3 vs Typhoon, who won?" – which made me smile.

It was a much shorter return leg as I had the benefit of that strong southerly wind, and after making a straight in approach and putting YL back to bed, I was still in time for that Wedding dinner later in the evening!

Blackpool

As I turned final for the third time at Rossall Field making my second approach to runway 02 (I'd already tried an approach to R28 which didn't work out either) I glanced over my shoulder to see that, reassuringly, I had at least 10 litres of fuel left before I was coming down one way or another.

Yep, it was turning out to be one of those days...

The idea of taking my little AX3 into Blackpool International Airport had been germinating for some time and it had actually been a great afternoon for the trip out. I'd elected to take Harriet on a long overdue familiarisation sortie to check out the new café there, but it was also an attractive destination anyway as I'd not flown in to Blackpool for a couple of years.

Cursing under my breath as I washed the expensive evidence of my inability to refuel from my hands, I made the necessary calls for PPR and to arrange parking. I was also aware that Blackpool had some ATC restrictions due to staff shortages, so I wanted to plan my arrival and departure times with these in mind.

Upon my arrival I noticed that the field, was busy with lots of club aircraft out of the hangar and lots of aviation being planned in a clubhouse decorated with a fair smattering of steaming cups. It was a stunning day, a bit of a breeze but nice and sunny. And, dare I say it, almost warm...

"Winter is finally over. Fact!" was the optimistic thought that shot through my brain.

NB – please remember what I've said before about suffixing a statement with the word, fact, right? It's automatically indisputable. Even if you find a contradictory reference on Wikipedia, that well-known platform of indisputable, unverifiable 'facts'.

As usual, I digress.

Backtracking runway 28 I turned and waited at the threshold observing the landing traffic on 02. The radio chirped to life: "Danny you've got plenty of time to go if you want," announced Andy. So, after a further visual scan I pushed the throttle to the stop and Harriet and I escaped our earthly bonds once more.

Realising that Blackpool would be on R28 (because of the westerly wind) I decided to head for Poulton VRP hoping to get routed for a right base join. Approaching Poulton, I contacted Blackpool Approach on 119.950. They were quite busy, but after a couple of "Golf Yankee Lima standby" responses, I was indeed asked to join right base behind a Cessna on downwind and was instructed to report visual and "follow the Cessna as number two".

This was great, except for one thing.

Where was that bloody Cessna? I'd never approached Blackpool from the north before and had no idea what landmarks to look for to help me locate the traffic. So, after hours (alright seconds) of scanning the sky in front of me, I spotted the Cessna slightly below and crossing right to left:

"Blackpool Approach, target in sight; I'm too close for missiles, switching to guns."

Ok, that's not quite the call I made, but it did feel a bit like a Top Gun sortie, as I swooped in behind the 'target' to join right base.

Turning final for the massive 1.8km long runway 28 immediately reminded me of the runway perspective training during my NPPL course. It's a long wide runway (probably wide enough for me to land Yankee Lima across, I must try that one day...) so I needed to remain aware that my eyes might play tricks on me. I also didn't want to touchdown on the numbers and then have to 'drive' over a mile to the apron.

I landed just beyond the numbers.

"D'oh!" as Homer Simpson would say.

Nothing I could do now except taxy as fast as possible whilst feeling the eyes of the pilot of the PA28 behind me boring into me.

So, I taxied fast.

Very fast.

In fact, I taxied so fast that I felt the nosewheel going 'light' quite a few times and had to touch the brakes more than once to prevent an accidental take-off without clearance from ATC!

Honest guv, I had at least one wheel on the ground at all times...

Pushing sneaky thoughts of taking off to get there quicker from my mind, I eventually reached the Delta taxiway and was helpfully guided to the parking by the ATCO. I find it a major stress reliever when ATC offer this facility to new or infrequent visitors, so full marks to Blackpool ATC for that.

After shutting down I was escorted into the café adjacent to the hangar where I paid my landing fee and enjoyed a very tasty bacon barm and coffee. As I sat there munching away, I reflected that I was lucky I had remembered my high-vis as the 'elf and safety police at Blackpool will not let you get away with dangerously walking around in 'normal' clothing.

On the apron at Blackpool with the tower (the other one) in the background and an Air Ambulance departing above my head...

I enjoyed the view from the café, as just next door there is an offshore oil rig helicopter which comes and goes and is always fascinating to watch but all too soon, I was ready to go and take Harriet back into the skies once more.

Having booked out and agreed an intersection take-off with ATC (as I really don't need a space shuttle landing sized runway for take-off in Harriet), I strapped in and began my checks. At this point I realised I'd forgotten to pre-programme Blackpool ATIS (127.200) into my radio and to compound this, I couldn't remember how to switch out of memory recall mode which entailed much button pressing and cursing in the cockpit.

Happily, I did eventually work it out and have since ensured I can actually change the radio frequency to anything, rather than relying on the frequencies that I have prestored.

Don't forget, kids, every flight is a learning opportunity!

The Blackpool ATCO cleared me to taxi to the Delta Two hold and when I got there, having already asked for runway 31, I was cleared to cross 28 and backtrack 31. There I was held while other traffic departed 28, but it gave me the opportunity to take some nice photos from the runway.

Patiently waiting clearance to take-off on Blackpool's runway 31

After take-off I flew a route that took me over my sister's house, and waggled Harriet's wings for her and her mother-in-law, before heading directly back to Rossall. Which brings me back to the start of this chapter. The wind had got up a little and couldn't seem to decide if it was westerly or north westerly. It was also gusting quite unpredictably too.

Initially I had tried an approach to 02 but got it all wrong, despite coming in with plenty of speed, and so I elected to go-around. Throttling up and glancing at the windsock I noted that the wind was now at 90 degrees to the runway. Grinning at my ingenuity, I repositioned for an approach to 28, directly into wind.

Or so I thought – if only life was so easy…

As I approached the hedge, I flew through a huge wind gradient and sunk about 30 feet. I applied power and stabilised the approach but by this point I could see the leaves on the hedge at the end of the runway a little too clearly and so I pushed the throttle forwards again and climbed away.

Stealing another glance at the windsock it was now more NNW again so I repositioned Harriet and I for 02 - again. Happily, this time I was finally able to make an acceptable approach and landed, but not after wondering how many times I would have to do this and how long 10 litres of fuel would last on take-off power…

Back in the clubhouse one of my club mates had inevitably noticed and whilst smiling at me quipped "did you work out which runway you prefer yet?"

Powerless to Do Anything

It was around the end of May 2019 that I first started to notice it. Of course, I tried to deny it and pretend it wasn't there, but there was no escaping the fact that YL was acting extremely lethargically on take-off. The first time this happened I put this down to extremely deep tread marks on the runway (the main runway was being extended at the time) that had slowed down my little caster-sized wheels during acceleration. I was also two-up and had the equivalent of a small oil refinery's worth of fuel onboard.

The next couple of flights I was solo, and flying with much less fuel so, naturally I put the lazy take-off performance down to the tractor marks, not anything to do with the engine.

Around a month later, as the nights were getting lighter and the optimism of the summer holidays with their long evening flights were tantalisingly close, there was no ignoring it.

"I can smell oil when you're climbing," Kaz muttered almost apologetically under her breath.

The truth was, I could too.

In fact, it had been bothering me for about five minutes, and I'd already turned back towards the airfield, and reduced the cruise speed.

Eyes flicking from engine RPM to CHT and EGT temperature gauges incessantly, whilst also trying to keep a good lookout, and listening keenly to the engine note, we returned to Rossall and landed on 02 without further problems.

Parking near the hangar, it was time to take a look at the hitherto, perfectly reliable Rotax 503 mounted precariously on the top of the fusetube at the very front of Harriet.

It was then that my smile dropped, as I realised what I was seeing.

Oil.

Sticky, black oil.

Oil on the HT leads.

Oil on the leading edge.

Oil on the windscreen.

Oil on the tail plane and rudder.

Oil everywhere.

'Oh dear' was the crushing thought that went through my mind. More truthfully, I actually used an extremely versatile word of Anglo-Saxon origin, often used by people to replace the 'dear' part in 'oh dear' in times of stress, but that's probably not what you want to read right now…

Still I'm nothing if not an optimist, so I started to inspect the engine to try and understand where the oil was coming from. I couldn't see any sign from the gearbox, the only place on a two-stroke where there is a reservoir of oil, and with no other obvious signs of where it was coming from, I did the obvious thing and turned it over to the wisdom of the internet.

My post read:

"Anyone experienced anything like this? Rotax 503 bit down on power (only getting 6400rpm) and some black sticky oil being sprayed on rear cylinder/leads and top of wing? No sign of gearbox leak and no obvious leaks I can see, apart from rear exhaust port is quite oily too? Any ideas on things to check?"

I also, helpfully, included some photographs of the engine to show pictures of the bits I was struggling to describe.

Never have I received such a flood of interaction on a Facebook post before! The replies included several things for me to check, some more helpful than others, ranging in usefulness from:

"Head gasket?"

"It does sound like a leaky exhaust gasket - though that doesn't explain the apparent lack of power. Do check prop pitch."

To the more unlikely

"Glow plugs are not tight."

"Not sure how a failed head gasket (an O-ring) can cause oil spray. It's surrounded by a water jacket and the usual symptom of failure would be losing coolant."

Rotax 503 engines do not have glow plugs and are not water-cooled, so I felt fairly happy discounting both of the above contributions and focussing on the lack of compression suggestions. One of which, in retrospect was bang on, but more on that later.

I'd decided to try changing the spark plugs, since this particular set had been in and out about three or four times, and the crush washers on them are only designed to seal once. When I took a look, this seemed promising as all around the number two plug on the PTO cylinder was lots of oil with nothing further forwards. I'd also had a conversation with Simon from Eccleston Aviation, who had suggested it might be the CHT sensor causing the plug not to seal properly against the cylinder head.

So, four new plugs, and some crush washers to try and seal the plug ports properly were promptly installed, and after torqueing everything correctly and cleaning oil off from every surface I could find, I nervously wheeled YL out and chocked the wheels.

I was really hoping it was that simple.

Strapped in and ready, I called "clear prop!"

As she always does (these days), she fired first time and I immediately set idle to around 3000rpm. After a minute or two to let the engine warm up, and a quick glance around to check it was safe, I increased the power slowly to take-off power.

This always feels wrong when you are static. The whole airframe is rocking and pulling and straining to go, and it can't. It behaves like an angry chained up beast, yearning for the sky, which was apt, as that was how I felt too at that moment.

The engine was screaming at full power, and I was thinking to myself 'are the chocks OK? Are they going to hold?' My seatbelt was on, I checked the tightness, I was watching the temps and I had an eye on the mags – JUST IN CASE.

A quick glance at the tachometer.

6700RPM.

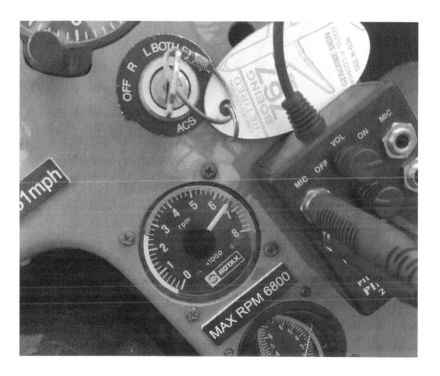

Max RPM and everything is shaking. I HATE ground runs...

Oh! I wasn't expecting that. Could that really be it? A simple spark plug change?

No.

No, that wasn't it.

And it was going to end up being far more costly to repair than a simple spark plug change.

I should've known better. Bloody stupid optimist.

Anyway, at this moment in time I felt a little elation and so at the next opportunity a couple of days later I decided to fly some circuits to check the engine again whilst remaining in safe gliding distance of the airfield.

It was on climb out for the second circuit that I noticed the RPM drop. 6100RPM on climb out was way down on where it had been previously, and she just felt, well, really sluggish. So, a quick tight circuit was in order and I soon had YL lined up for runway 02 nicely, and made a very nice touchdown which I managed to half smile about despite the circumstances. I always find that there's something really satisfying about a well-executed landing.

However, my fleeting moment of joy was to prove short lived, as things went from simply disappointing to expensive and disappointing.

As I approached the hangar to spin round and park up, the left main punctured.

It's almost like someone was trying to keep me on the ground. I mean I'd only just replaced those tyres and tubes a mere six hours ago, and as that thought rang through my mind I remembered James' comment when I was excitedly detailing the bargain of the century I had just bought from the online tyre company.

"That's very cheap!"

Yeah, cheap and poorly manufactured.

Then to cap it all I managed to scratch my lovely new car with the wingtip when I was manoeuvring YL to refit the new tyres I'd sourced.

Twice.

Not a great day...

Who said this aviation lark is supposed to be fun though, eh?

In fact, at this point I was seriously considering the wisdom of a somewhat disillusioned person who allegedly once said:

"If it flies, floats or fornicates, always rent it – it's cheaper in the long run!"

Being a detail kind of guy, despite the obvious loss of power on climb out, I went for a look around the airframe to check for any sign of oil on Harriet. And there sadly, on the wing, tail and fin were oil spots. Again. I looked around the engine and there was no obvious sign of where the oil had come from, but there were the spots of oil on the HT leads into the mag cylinder again.

I'd had enough though by this point, and so based on this hitherto unnoticed overdeveloped unlucky streak, I decided to put Harriet to bed and come back to try again another day.

I returned to Harriet within the week with the intention of performing a series of ground runs to ascertain if I could understand what was going on. In total I did three, and they revealed a very strange pattern. Initially I would start up, and when I went to full power she gave me 6400/6500RPM. But as the engine warmed, this fell back to about 6200RPM. This pattern confused me, because I figured if it was a gas blow by on the spark plug port (as I'd thought) this would be more consistent. The only thing I could think of was that perhaps as the engine heated up, some area that was blocked by oil/generic gunge was getting hot enough to allow gas through.

Suitably confused and no further forward I retired to the lounge and indulged myself with a nice cup of tea.

Two days later and as is all too common in the North West it was yet another non-flying day. However, I was back at the field and, in true Baldrick fashion, after conversations with people far more knowledgeable than me, I had come armed with a cunning plan. It went something like this:

1. Remove the two plugs that have CHT sensors on them.
2. Apply thermic compound on the plug thread and then refit to see if that stemmed the oil loss.

Simple enough eh?

No.

With the spark plug removed, I opened the packet of thermic compound and started to apply it. I don't know if you've ever seen or touched this stuff but it reminded me of that current (depending on when you read this) craze that seems to be the obsession of every pre-teen in the country.

Slime.

You know that stuff that the enterprising corporations utilising subliminal messaging of some kind have managed to convince all kids that they need, want and must have. My youngest daughter can in fact sometimes resemble a child version of Golem in fact, from The Lord of the Rings fame, when you put a pot of slime in front of her.

"We wants it we does... GIVE IT TO US!"

I degress; back to my broken engine.

There I was, happily refitting it, after gunging it up with the slime, erm, thermic compound. By now this was something I'd done tons of times, when the torque wrench clicked unexpectedly early, in fact wayyyy too early.

Is there a more sickening sound? I'm not sure there was at that moment in my life. Gingerly I removed the spark plug socket, and there, sticking proudly out of the top of my engine, at an extremely odd angle, was a spark plug.

I'd cross threaded it.

At this point I decided that the best, and indeed only sensible course of action, was to go to the pub.

So, I went to the pub.

Unsurprisingly, when I awoke the next day nursing a slightly sore head, it dawned on me that this had not actually solved my engine problems.

A few frantic texts back and forth between Simon (from Ecclestone Aviation) and me, soon, however filled me with some hope as he explained that he could fit a recoil to the spark plug port and it would all be ok and probably not such an expensive mistake after all. As it happened the engine was coming up to 50hrs and was due a decoke. So, arrangements were made and over the coming week I carefully removed the broken powerplant from Harriet ready for Simon to collect.

There was still the lingering mystery of the power loss though...

My Rotax 503, waiting...

A couple of weeks later, Simon arrived to collect my engine and after a cup of tea in the clubhouse, he took a look and within, literally seconds he said "I can see why you've had the power loss."

Intrigued, and also a little worried, I followed him into the hangar to see what the problem was.

Pointing at the problem, he told me: "You've had a seizure on the PTO cylinder, take a look." And I did.

It was obvious, now that I saw it, that the side of the piston was all black and scorched, presumably from where the hot gases had been escaping and causing the cylinder to lose some compression, and thus power. Writing this chapter some weeks later, I recalled another comment on the Facebook post I had made asking about power loss.

"Remove the exhaust manifold and see if you can see a join in any of the piston rings - if so the ring stop has failed the rings have rotated damaging the cylinder bores. Blow by gasses causing the leaking symptom."

When I looked inside the engine, it resembled exactly this kind of problem. Ten out of ten to Paul, who suggested this was the issue all along!

The End of the Road?

So, there I was, in the middle of an, albeit fair to average, Lancashire summer with an aircraft that was stuck on the ground awaiting a phone call from Simon, to tell me if my engine was salvageable.

Characteristically I was optimistic as Simon had pointed out that it hadn't stopped and indeed had run since the seizure several times, so we were both hopeful he would be able to hone the inside of the cylinder and that would be that.

It was a Monday when I got the text.

"Too deep to hone, sorry mate."

The accompanying photo, illustrated the message that Simon's text was conveying.

The scorched and scratched inside of the damaged cylinder

Going from bad to worse, it turned out it would need boring out. This would also mean that both cylinders would need doing to keep the engine balanced, and that would in turn mean two new pistons, instead of one. To put it in simple terms, it meant spending well over £1000, and that is a lot of money to sink into an aeroplane, that however much I love her, was only worth around £2500 in flying condition.

I needed some time to think.

Thinking entailed asking flying friends about 503 engines that might be available. Chasing down rumours of available engines, and frantically scouring the AFORS website almost every waking moment of the next week or so, while I tried to come up with a plan of what to do. I asked Kaz what she thought, and she offered the following advice, "I think you should grieve, get over it and sell YL and move on."

And that is what I was almost going to do until I had another Baldrick moment.

What if I could find a donor engine? It seemed impossible because, the only engine I'd seen recently on AFORS was a complete dual ignition 503, and that in itself was £1000.

I'd even already started thinking about what aeroplane to replace Harriet with... I know, I know, how could I? But the fact remains that hope was thin on the ground at this point and I wanted to keep on flying. It was doubly frustrating because I did not want this story to end with me selling Harriet for scrap or parts.

Ironically, it was about this time whilst browsing AFORS for the four millionth time that day that I remembered the Rans S6 503 I had seen advertised. It wasn't too expensive, had recently had the decoke done on its engine, looked to be in good condition, and I also remembered the advert contained this precious line:

"Comes with a spare 503DCI engine with gearbox."

This was unbelievably perfect: I could fly the Rans and use the spare engine to rebuild Harriet to flying condition, before selling her and finishing this story in the way I had originally envisioned. James also suggested that it would be good to convert the Rans to a 582 as well to take it to 450kg, so that would be another project for the winter to consider.

148

But first I had an aircraft to purchase.

I flicked through my text messages to find the conversation I had been having with the current owner previously and punched out a quick text message.

"Hi again – have you still got the Rans for sale?"

And then as an afterthought.

"And you mention in the advert there is a spare engine included. Is it serviceable? Hours? Thanks."

Almost immediately the owner replied. And it was not the reply I was looking for either.

"Hi, currently has a deposit on it, but will let you know if it falls through. Thanks."

So, that was another avenue that was, at least temporarily, closed off to me. I was seriously running out of ideas at this point and wondered what I would have to do to get my aeroplane back into the skies. The Rans had seemed like a perfect solution, I mean, who sells an aircraft with a spare engine? Let alone the right one for Harriet? I was gutted.

In the depths of my despair I recalled Simon suggesting it might be an idea to ask the BMAA about fitting a fan-cooled 503 to Harriet, instead of the free air-cooled type, as he explained most of the cooling on a free air-cooled one goes to the rear cylinder due to the way the air scoop works. Indeed, when I looked through the paperwork the last engine failure was on the PTO cylinder as well.

Realising that this would increase the options available to me, and also improve the reliability of my aeroplane, I contacted the BMAA Tech Office to enquire if this would be feasible. Their reply gave me something to think about as they suggested it should be OK but I may suffer a slight weight penalty and would also need to get the weight and balance redone on Harriet if I went down this route. Food for thought.

Desperation at this point was at an all-time high, and so I fired up the laptop and wrote my own 'Desperately Seeking Susan" advert on AFORS (sorry for the 80s reference there).

Rotax 503 Wanted

Rotax 503 or 503 parts required (serviceable PTO cylinder at least). Free air-cooled or fan-cooled considered.

And then I waited.

It was the next day that Jeff first texted me.

"Hello Danny. Just a reply to your advert on AFORS re 503. I have just taken a running 503 points ignition out of my MiniMax plus I've another points ignition engine stripped down with a main bearing fault, most of the parts are boxed up. Not sure if it's any good for you. Regards."

I replied and ascertained that the cylinders were the same as mine but the heads were different due to them only having one spark plug port (which was a shame given my spark plug debacle). I wasn't sure if this would work or not so I asked Simon and waited for a reply.

Not being blessed with limitless patience, and anxious to get things moving, later that day I decided I would simply contact anyone on AFORS who had advertised a 503 in the last six months. Dual ignition or single ignition, I contacted them all.

Unfortunately, most of them came back and said they had sold their engines already, although one gentleman did have a single ignition one that he did not know what he wanted to do with, and invited me to make him an offer. I said I would get back to him when I had worked out what a fair price would be.

Then, Simon texted me back to let me know that we only needed the barrels (cylinders) and pistons from Jeff's engine as they are the same as the DCDI ones.

Was that hope on the horizon?

Hope on the Horizon

This unexpected turn of events led to some frantic texting on my part trying to ascertain would they indeed work with my engine? What condition were they in? Could I have some pictures?

And then the big one…

"How much do you want for them?"

Jeff came back to me pretty quickly and said, "how does £80 + PP sound?" To me it sounded like music to my ears. After the £1000+ quote for brand new pistons and necessary cylinder boring, £80 sounded almost free.

So as soon as I got the pictures, I sent them on to Simon and asked his opinion which was that, they looked OK, but it was difficult to tell from photos. He said they sounded an absolute bargain at £80 and then as we got talking about who was sending them, he said "I know Jeff, he's a good bloke." which gave me a bit more comfort.

So, with that nugget of comfort I made my decision and decided to go for it.

I can't adequately describe to you my feelings of apprehension curiously mixed with hope. Up until now I had written off ever flying Harriet again, as the cost to put her back into the sky seemed far too prohibitive. It's not that I couldn't afford it, but it just didn't seem like a wise decision financially, but then again, who ever said owning a plane is financially a good decision?

See my previous comment about renting…

Jeff and I agreed I would make payment once he had posted, which again, given I had never met him, increased my trust in these days of internet scams.

Jeff posted the parts a few days later via recorded delivery guaranteed 24 hours, but for some reason I missed the bit that said "next working day" and therefore they didn't arrive on the Saturday as I had hoped. Still, I had plenty of other jobs to get on with that I had left until I knew the engine was going to be sorted.

I wanted the engine to look as good as possible; sure not classic car concourse good, but still nice and clean, so I decided to replace some of the hardware used to attach the engine ancillaries.

I was in the hangar measuring up the propeller bolts when I bumped into James, who asked what I was doing. "I've come to measure the prop bolts to make sure I get exactly the right ones!" I announced proudly.

"Oh right, have you got a Vernier?"

"A what?"

"A Vernier gauge, for measuring the bolts."

"Erm, no, I just put them next to a tape measure mate."

Cue James reaching deep into his seemingly inexhaustible supply of incredulous expressions to deploy yet another 'look' that told me I still had much to learn about engineering.

However, having sourced the new propeller bolts, I still nearly managed to buy the wrong ones. I was going to get stainless steel thinking they would last longer, but at the last minute waited to speak to James. "Don't try and be clever and get stainless steel mate, I once saw a Shadow taxying in and when the engine stopped the propeller just dropped to the floor." The guy had just replaced his propeller bolts with stainless steel ones, they had all sheared in flight and the only thing keeping the propeller in place had been the force generated by the thrust!

Phew, close call, cadmium-coated mild steel it is then!

Exhaust components were next up: new manifold bolts, exhaust springs (for holding the three parts of the exhaust together) and I also decided to get the exhaust blasted and painted as it was looking a little tired. This meant stripping the exhaust down into its component parts, but this gave me something interesting to figure out: how to remove the existing exhaust springs in a non-destructive fashion?

Google to the rescue – using the following self-explanatory search terms: "how to remove exhaust springs under tension."

This led me to a neat little trick using sacrificial cable-ties to unhook the spring without damaging either the spring or the fitting.

Cool, eh?

The exhaust came apart easily enough after I had snipped off about seven miles of lockwire around the exhaust springs – guess the previous owner really didn't want the exhaust to fall apart mid-flight... So that was set aside ready for blasting and painting.

The next job I was looking at was the air scoop as this needed improvement in a couple of ways: cosmetic (I wanted to paint it black to match the new more subtle exhaust colour I was going for), and also practical, the cooling to the front cylinder really isn't as efficient as it could be.

You'll also recall I'd had my fair share of tyre problems and had ended up replacing the two main wheel tyres barely a month after I had done them due to poor quality tyres. I figured that now would be a good time to strip the nose wheel down and inspect the tube/tyre just to be safe. I needn't have worried though; it was fine - probably due to my excellent 'wheelieing' technique after landing meaning that it barely gets used.

Well, that's what I tell myself anyway!

Back to the Skies Once More?

A few days later, and Simon had received the pistons and cylinders from Jeff. I was on tenterhooks (whatever that actually means…) as I anticipated every possible outcome apart from actually being able to fly my aeroplane ever again. However, after a few days, I sent a tentative text:

"Morning Simon – hope you enjoyed you break. Have you got an update on my engine please? Weather looks good this weekend so I'm keen to get flying if possible."

Then I waited – for what seemed like an eternity, but in actual fact was just one minute.

"Just a few more checks. I'm going to try and get it finished this morning," came the reply I was hoping for!

So, a few hours (and text messages) later I set off for Preston to collect my newly rebuilt engine, something I had seriously doubted I would be able to say, only a few weeks previously.

I had also been hoping to collect my newly repainted exhaust too, but unfortunately it was not ready, and it was a bank holiday weekend, with, ironically, superb weather forecast all weekend.

So close…

However, George, the helpful owner of Fast Line Coatings, offered to ensure it was done Monday morning, even though it was a bank holiday. This, I reasoned, would actually ensure that I had plenty of time over the weekend to reinstall my engine and ancillaries and check everything properly.

No one wants an engine to fall off mid-flight, as it tends to limit the range and also alters the handling characteristics somewhat...

And so began the process of rebuilding my aircraft, and trying to remember where everything came from, and in what order to put everything back. It wasn't actually too bad as (and here's a top tip) James had recommended I take lots of photos of everything as I was taking it off, which really helped to ensure I got things back the right way up and in the right order etc.

By the end of the Sunday, Harriet was complete, minus the air scoop and exhaust thanks to assistance from James, Mark and Andy from the club – all whom have vastly more experience than me with engines and have managed to stop me from doing something stupid on more than one occasion.

The following day, I collected the exhaust and by teatime (southerners - it's a northern phrase for the meal in the evening, not something you drink) she was sitting outside waiting to be run. By then, I'd drained the old fuel out and replaced it with a new mix of 50:1 and checked and rechecked everything I could think of.

Nothing else for it – time to flick the mags!

I walked around Harriet like an expectant father, checking the airframe and most importantly, the engine, that everything looked right and felt tight. I'd chocked the wheels, and pointed her down the open field – just in case.

I strapped in, and began my STAMP checks whilst Andy pulled the prop around by hand a few times.

Then there was nothing left to check.

"Clear Prop, Clear Prop!"

I paused for a heartbeat, and then turned the key.

The starter motor whined and the prop turned.

My vast audience (well Andy and Brian) looked on.

Would she fire?

Would she ever!

After turning all of two or three seconds – she burst into life and settled happily at around 3000RPM.

A huge smile spread across my face, as I realised everything was going to be ok. I ran the engine up to temperature and increased power to about 4000RPM, carefully watching the CHT temperatures before turning her off and letting her cool down. I repeated this procedure again and then, with no adverse effects noted, decided the next test would be a full power acceleration test down the runway.

As I thumbed the PTT I gleefully announced, "Golf Yankee Lima, entering and back tracking runway 02 for fast taxi." and then gunned the engine to get moving.

All the while watching the CHT temperatures.

Lining up and a quick pre-take-off check completed, there was nothing else for it.

I pushed the throttle to full power and as we started to accelerate, flicked my eyes to the tacho.

6500RPM was the reward my expectant gaze received.

My eyes dropped to the CHT gauges.

All good there too. So, after about five seconds at full power, and Harriet rapidly approaching flying speed, I reduced power and flared the wings to slow us down to a crawl.

"F*** it, I'm going for it" I grinned to myself.

I turned Harriet around and announced to no one in particular "Rossall Traffic, Golf Yankee Lima backtracking runway 02 for immediate departure."

It felt so good to say those words again.

Turning at the top of the runway, I took a quick look around the cockpit again and did my mental last checks, mags on, trim set for take-off, temps looking good, and windsock is ok. Nothing in front of me, and no reason not to go.

"Golf Yankee Lima, taking off runway 02."

This was a moment I'd thought I'd never experience again in this, my first love, in aeroplane terms (sorry Kaz), I savoured it for five seconds, and then with nothing else to check, I pushed the throttle gradually to the stop.

Full power achieved = check.

RPM looks good = check.

No reason to not continue the take-off = check.

Rotate…

And off we went.

Moments before touchdown at Troutbeck in the Lake District - photo courtesy of Roger Savage

Back in the Saddle

In mid-July 2020 Harriet came full circle and completed one final training flight. That flight was my FI(R) flight test, which happily I passed. This is a fitting end to the story, given that she has flown countless training flights and flight tests during the 90s and early 2000s when in her prime. It is also somewhat apt, as the examiner who conducted my initial GST six years previously, Chris Copple, flew his first Flight Instructor test in Harriet.

She has logged over 3600 hours on her airframe now and still gives me as much joy to fly as I'm sure she has all the owners and pilots who have contributed to this book, as well as the many others who have flown her.

As I embark on my new career as a part-time flight instructor with James at Attitude Airsports, I am excited to have the opportunity to fly some beautifully built modern aeroplanes such as the Nynja and EuroFox. I am however, also certain that I will never get bored of taking a slow bimble in the calm evening sky in my first aeroplane.

Acknowledgements

Aside from my family and friends who have encouraged me and generally been supportive, there are several people without whose contributions this book would have been considerably shorter and less interesting. In no particular order - actually that's a lie, it's based on the order of my email folder:

Thanks to Graeme Park for all the RAF information and the photographs he provided, and also the pristine AX3 brochure! To Bill Sherlock who fact checked the history sections and contributed some lovely anecdotes from his time developing and gaining the certification for the AX3 from the CAA. A nod to Bill Schmidt who responded to my email request for information on a story he wrote for the New York Times over 35 years ago and a big thanks to Tom Garnham for selling Yankee Lima to me and enabling me to have all the adventures I've had so far.

Ben Ashman, Terry Clark, Adam Bedborough, Graham Richardson, Dave Wallington, Anna Casey and Paul Higgins: thanks for your own contributions both large and small to add to the colour of the story of Yankee Lima. Tony Mcdowell (cover photo), Roger Savage and Gavin Carr provided some cracking photographs of Yankee Lima in action. James Walker, Simon Worthington and my club mates who were patient, and fixed my mistakes, when I was not.

A big thank you to Chris Copple and Marcus Furniss for teaching me to fly, and to Matt and Clare Roach who bought me that flight simulator session that reignited my desire to learn to fly.

Thanks to Sarah Northwood for inspiring me to attempt to write a book and to Norman Burr for providing research and articles from the vaults of Microlight Flying magazine. A huge thanks to Geoff Hill for his guidance on writing and style, for proof-reading the manuscript and providing editorial feedback, and for encouraging me to write when I wasn't sure if I could. And a big shout out to Karlene Petitt, herself an accomplished author and pilot of grown up planes, for her advice on the cover design and how to write an engaging synopsis.

Thanks to all three of my daughters; Izzy, Millie and Elektra for, at some time or other, all feigning some kind of passable interest in their Dad's hobby.

Finally, thanks to my Mum and Dad for raising me with some kind of ambition and drive and to Kaz, my patient wife, for her enthusiasm for life and encouragement of every mad scheme I come up with, for editing the grammatical incompetence out of this book and, most importantly, for still being my patient wife...

References

1. 27/7/2020, all-aero.com/index.php/56-planes-v-w/11768-weedhopper-of-utah-jc-24-weedhopper.
2. Schmidt. W.A, (1981) 27/7/2020, ULTRALIGHT PLANES: FLYING VERSION OF THE 5-CENT CIGAR, NYTimes, June 14, 1981 - WILLIAM E. SCHMIDT - www.nytimes.com/1981/06/14/us/ultralight-planes-flying-version-of-the-5-cent-cigar.html.
3. 27/7/2020, www.aero-news.net/index.cfm?do=main.textpost&id=ba2527a7-0f0e-4b5e-afd5-d8546d677ba5.
4. Scott. D.A, (2007) Chotia 460 Aircraft Engine Operation Manual.
5. 27/7/2020, en.wikipedia.org/wiki/Chotia_Weedhopper.
6. Sherlock. B, (circa 1995) Original Cyclone Airsports AX3 Brochure.
7. 27/7/2020, afors.com/aircraftView/40746/Cyclone-AX3/503-.
8. Grimstead. B, (1995) Cyclone AX3 Review, p. 22, Pilot Magazine (October).
9. Burr. N, (2015) First Principles: The Official Biography of Keith Duckworth OBE.
10. (1994) Whistles in the Wires, Microlight Flying Magazine (November/December).
11. Dewhurst. P, (1994) Lady and the Tramp, Microlight Flying Magazine (May/June).

12.   27/7/2020, You Bet! - series 8, episode 9, 22/4/1995 John Regis, Jessica Martin, Bobby George, Billy Pearce - www.youtube.com/watch?v=aFxr-DcEnls&t=10s.

13.   Bremner. D, (2019) Bristol Scout 1264: Rebuilding Granddad's Aircraft'.

In addition to the above references, the following sources were also consulted (last accessed 27/7/2020) and used to further my understanding and build a network of people who had been involved in the AX3 from the earlier days of microlighting:

14.   www.pprune.org/archive/index.php/t-611598.html.

15.   www.bmaa.org/the-bmaa/bmaa-history/bmaa-history-1994.

16.   ulav8r.com/cyclone_ax3.htm.

17.   www.microlightforum.com/showthread.php?13011-Cyclone-AX3-evaluation-by-RAF.

Glossary

AEF – Air Experience Flight, the units of the RAF that look after Air Cadet flying and sometimes make them sick...

AFI – Assistant Flying Instructor, the first step on the ladder of a flying instructor. This rating is achieved by passing a Flight Instructor course and then a test with a Flight Instructor Examiner. This is now superseded by the FI(R) rating which is very similar.

AFORS – a website where bored pilots go to look at aeroplanes they can't afford to buy.

Ailerons – moveable surfaces at the end of the wings that when moved via the stick, induce a roll causing the aircraft to bank, derived from a French word for the extremities of a bird's wings, for those who are interested.

AP1919 – the rules and regulations that are used to administer the Air Cadets.

ATC – Air Training Corp, or Air Cadets. Also a term for Air Traffic Control, a form of ATS.

ATCO – Air Traffic Control Officer, person who works in ATC, skilled in patience, Extra-sensory perception and understanding unintelligible R/T transmissions.

ATIS – Automatic Terminal Information Service, a radio broadcast that gives you the weather, runway in use and a few other useful bits of information read by the bloke that used to read the speaking clock back in the day.

ATS – Air Traffic Services, an umbrella term for the different types of R/T service you get at different airfields or indeed in the air.

Base – the fourth leg of the circuit flown perpendicular towards the runway immediately before you turn Final and line up for approach to the runway.

BMAA – British Microlight Aircraft Association the administrative body for all things microlighting in the UK.

CAA – Civil Aviation Authority the administrative body for all things aviation in the UK, sometimes referred to as the Campaign Against Aviation.

Circuit (Pattern) – the route flown around an airfield prior to landing, this is a set procedure so that every pilot knows what every other pilot is doing, at least that's the theory…

CFI – Chief Flying Instructor, the title generally adopted by the most experienced, senior and/or owner of a flying school.

CHT – Cylinder Head Temperature, if this gets too hot, it's really bad.

Climb out – the first leg of the circuit as you climb away from the runway.

Crosswind – the second leg of the circuit you turn onto after climb out, that takes you towards the start of the downwind leg.

DCDI – Dual Capacitor Discharge Ignition, the way the spark is generated and sent to the spark plug by the engine.

Downwind – the third leg of the circuit flown parallel to the runway and in the opposite direction to take-off with the wind behind you, hence downwind.

Elevators – no not a lift to take you to your hotel room, but a moveable surface on the tail of the aircraft that control the pitch of the aircraft.

Fanstop – what the instructor calls on the radio to announce to the ATS that he is removing the power from the aeroplane to see if the student can cope, also referred to as EFATO practice meaning Engine Failure After Take-Off.

Final – the last leg of the circuit where you are lined up with the runway and descending, hopefully, towards it.

Fusetube – the big aluminium tube running front to back that everything on my AX3 hangs off.

Google – really? Ok, a search engine (think index if you are not computer minded) on the internet…

Group A – larger aircraft that do not fall into the microlight category such as Piper Cherokee or Cessna 172, sometimes referred to as Spam Cans…

GST – General Skills Test, or the driving test for your pilot's license. Also, your last chance to get it wrong with an instructor there to save you in the other seat.

Knots – nautical miles per hour, roughly 1.15 statute miles per hour, derived from a nautical term as is much of our language.

Leading Edge – the front of the wing that generates a lot of the lift.

Mags or Magnetos – are the means by which electrical power is delivered to the spark plugs in the engine. It's the equivalent of the ignition on a car engine, not the plural of a comic book villain!

Master switch – is the switch that controls all auxiliary electrics within the aircraft, in my case, nothing, but on other aircraft this could include the radio, phone chargers, landing lights, beer fridges etc.

MATZ – Military Aerodrome Traffic Zone – a piece of airspace, generally used by fast jets, that it is recommended to ask permission to fly through it, although bizarrely that's not mandatory…

NPPL – National Private Pilot's License is a license that is issued to pilots and is valid only within UK airspace unless there is some other agreement in place. It is more restrictive than a full PPL and can only be exercised on certain types of aircraft e.g. Microlights.

Pitot tube – a small tube facing forwards into the airflow that feeds the air speed indicator which then converts this to a reading on the dial to give the pilot an idea of how fast he isn't flying.

PTO Cylinder – Power Take Off Cylinder, the one at the front where the driveshaft emerges to connect to the gearbox, or where the power is taken off! Simples.

PPR – Prior Permission Required, you need to ring to say you are coming, you can't just rock up and land.

PTT – Push to talk, the button in the cockpit that you, erm, push to talk to the ATS or another aircraft.

Reduction gearbox – Microlight engines rev high, in my case as high as 6800RPM. If the propeller were to be connected directly to the driveshaft the tips of the propeller, spinning much faster than the centre, would go supersonic. This creates a lot of noise and would also make them very brittle. The answer is to reduce the speed of the propeller by fitting a gearbox in between.

Rotax – a manufacturer of microlight engines.

Rotax 503 – a two-cylinder, two-stroke, inline, air-cooled microlight engine with twin ignition and twin carbs developing around 50 horsepower.

Rotax 582 – a two-cylinder, two-stroke, inline, air and water-cooled microlight engine developing around 65 horsepower, but not as good as my 503…

Rotax 912 – a four-cylinder, four-stroke, horizontally opposed water-cooled microlight engine developing around 80 or 100hp, complicated to look at, reliable to run.

R/T – Radio Telephony, the rather antiquated term used to describe the procedures we follow to talk to ground stations and other aircraft.

Rudder – controlled from the cockpit via pedals, this is used to keep the aircraft pointing in the direction in which it is travelling and prevent it from skidding in turns. Not primarily used for turning, like a ship, but in an emergency, e.g. if the ailerons were jammed, it could be, in theory, although I've never tried it.

Runway 02 – Runways are referred to by their magnetic heading to the nearest 10 degrees. So, a runway that is oriented towards the North on a heading of 020, becomes Runway 02. This helps pilots know which way to approach an airfield for landing.

Side-slipping – deliberately flying the aircraft out of balance to present the side of the fuselage to the oncoming airflow and thus increase the rate of descent. In the AX3 this is something approaching that of a double decker bus dropped from the sky.

TAF – Terminal Aerodrome Forecast is a forecast of weather at an aerodrome for a set period ahead usually 24 or 30 hours.

Tricycle Undercarriage – an arrangement of wheels under the aircraft that resembles a tricycle, as opposed to a conventional undercarriage such as the Spitfire or Thruster that have the centre wheel at the tail of the aircraft.

Trim Tab – a moveable control surface used to remove the aerodynamic forces from controls in flight so the pilot does not have to keep exerting force to do this and can kick back and have a cup of tea, kind of…

USAAF – United States Army Air Force, the precursor of the USAF which was formed after the Second World War, presumably formed to reduce the wear and tear on the A key on typewriters? The USAAF had a large number of airbases in the south east of the UK during the Second World War.

171

VRB – Variable so VRB/02 would mean wind from any direction at a speed of two knots.

VRP – visual reference point, a defined recognisable (sometimes) ground feature that you can use to report your position to an ATS unit.

Weight shift (or flex wing) Microlight – what you probably think of when someone says microlight. A sail or wing with a trike unit suspended beneath it. Control is achieved by pushing the wing left or right or pulling it in or out using a bar, thus moving the weight of the trike around beneath the pivot point. Ok, a kite with a lawnmower engine in it… (joking ☺.)

YL – Yankee Lima, the star of this book. Microlights, in fact, most small aircraft are often referred to by the last two letters of their Civil Aviation Authority registration mark, so G-MYYL becomes YL or Yankee Lima.

Two-Axis Microlight – A microlight aircraft that can only be controlled directly in 2-axis, pitch and yaw. The design of the wing ensures that when the aircraft is yawed it induces roll and thus the aeroplane turns.

Three-Axis Microlight – A microlight aircraft that flies and looks like a conventional aeroplane with controls that work in all three-axis, usually controlled via a stick for pitch and roll, and rudder pedals for yaw - the same arrangement that you would find in a Boeing 737 airliner.